Pres. 5/3/05

Be Delighted

A Tribute to Maureen Potter

Deirdre Purcell was born and brought up in Dublin. She had an eclectic set of careers, including acting at the Abbey Theatre, before she became a journalist and writer, winning awards for her work on the *Sunday Tribune*. Since 1991 she has published nine critically acclaimed novels, all of which have been bestsellers in Ireland. *Falling for a Dancer* was adapted into a popular four-part television mini-series, while *Love Like Hate Adore* was shortlisted for the prestigious Orange Prize. Her most recent novels for New Island are bestsellers *Marble Gardens* and *Last Summer in Arcadia*.

Deirdre Purcell lives in Dublin with her husband. She has two adult sons.

Be Delighted

A Tribute to

Maureen Potter

COMPILED AND EDITED BY

DEIRDRE PURCELL

NEW
ISLAND

Contents

Foreword by Jack O'Leary   ix

Part I   Entrance   1

Part II   How Did She Do It?   43

Part III   Going to the Panto   55

Part IV   The Brass   83

Part V   On stage   109

Part VI   Backstage   121

Part VII   An Enigma   157

Part VIII   Tommy the Theatre Cat   177

Part IX   Off-stage   183

Part X   That Was Then   211

Part XI   Exit   249

Author Index   267

Young Maureen on stage, 1959.

Maureen with Bobby the cat. Courtesy of George McFall

I think I could turn and live with animals, they are so placid and self-contained,
I stand and look at them long and long.

They do not sweat and whine about their condition,
They do not lie awake in the dark and weep for their sins,
They do not make me sick discussing their duty to God,
Not one is dissatisfied, not one is demented with the mania of owning things,
Not one kneels to another, nor to his kind that lived thousands of years ago,
Not one is respectable or unhappy over the whole earth.

WALT WHITMAN

Brendan Behan, who, if he was anything, was a Marxist humanist, objected very strongly to these lines from Walt Whitman's *Song of Myself.* Marxism did not have much time for animals, and neither did our natal Catholicism, since animals did not have immortal souls and were not candidates for salvation.

Of course, the lines are not to be interpreted as a considered statement by Whitman that animals are preferable to humans. All poetic expression is to some extent lyrical, expressing only the mood of the moment. And most poems are to some degree fictions: they change the circumstance in which the emotion is felt, however slightly.

But in any case, Whitman is more concerned with humans here than he is with animals, which he is using for contrast. And most of what he laments about humans is lamentable, even though it may demonstrate their superiority to mere animal existence.

ANTHONY CRONIN
Sunday Independent, 16 May 2004

Maureen and Jack, O'Connell Bridge. Courtesy of Jack O'Leary

Foreword

We got letters and Mass cards from all over the country, from Dingle to Donegal – and that nice man, Eamon Morrissey, told of a standing ovation in Tralee.

The past is the old man's friend and in my case, sitting here without her, the past is with her, filtered through the lens of our lives together.

My friend and army colleague, Jerry Fitzmaurice, approached me one day in 1940. 'I have an invitation to go to the Capitol next week. We will be going backstage. Would you like to come?' Little did I know then that the invite would change my life so dramatically.

I got my 'civvies' in order and met Jerry Fitzmaurice as arranged. He was in uniform, buttons shining, Sam Browne polished and gleaming. 'Are we going in uniform?' I asked.

'Certainly we are,' said Jerry. 'I'm hoping to persuade some of the performers to go to the bog and entertain the lads.' At that time, during the Emergency, as we called it, many army units were working on the bog, cutting turf to see us through the winter months.

So I changed back into uniform and we set out along the quays for the Capitol Theatre. We walked everywhere in those days; taxis were few and far between and, indeed, an army salary did not reach to such luxuries.

It was there in the Capitol I met Maureen Potter. I watched from the wings as she performed her number with the Capitol Orchestra: 'Little Mr Baggy Breeches' it was called: *And if you'll be my Sunday Fella, I'll patch up your breeches with Pink and with Yellow* ...

I was smitten.

I soon became her 'Sunday Fellow'. We went to see a film on a Sunday afternoon and then her mother, a lovely lady, gave us our tea. After tea, Mrs Potter went off to the pictures in the Fairview Grand so we had the house to ourselves. There was no TV then so we sat in the kitchen and listened to the wireless.

Cue Panto –

– *Oh no you didn't!*

– *Oh yes we did!*

We listened to *Sing Something Simple* and *Semprini Serenade*, and if you don't believe me, consult the *Radio Times* for the Sundays of 1940.

In fact, we were so intent on the wireless that we didn't get married until 1959.

The ceremony in the church at Fairview was very early; so early that the regular seven o'clock Mass-goers could be heard hammering on the door as we took our vows. (The groom's remark that they were trying to stop the marriage was not appreciated.) At the time, Maureen was appearing in *The Maureen Potter Show*, a weekly radio programme, and that 'big-hearted' producer Fred O'Donovan gave us a week off for a honeymoon in Kinsale.

It was on that honeymoon that Christy was born. He appeared on the radio programme each week after that as a typical 'Dubalin' child who got into all sorts of scrapes. I can assure you it was very hard work writing a new one for him each week, but I think Maureen's favourite Christy episode was 'Christy and the Balloons'.

In those days, if a child could be tempted into a shoe shop for a new pair of shoes, the owner rewarded him with a number of balloons. These extracts will not read too well in print without the Potter Dublin accent, in which, by common consent, they were hilarious. They speak of a Dublin of years ago, probably not too familiar to younger readers.

But to get back to Christy, as soon as he left the shop with his balloons, he rose into the air and floated away while his mother abused a policeman for not holding on to him: 'No, he's not floating down from a space ship – he's floating *up* from a *shoe shop* ...'

Chased by his anxious ma, Christy floated up O'Connell Street, on the wrong side of course, and hovered for a bit over Clerys, while his mother worried aloud to anyone who would listen: 'He'll never get in there with his Dublin accent'; and then: 'They'll think Mrs Guiney is running a Pawn shop!'

Nelson, of course, wasn't there when Christy crossed O'Connell Street towards the GPO, 'just when he could do some good for the country ...'

As he drifted onwards towards the Gresham Hotel his mother, alarmed now, just managed to keep pace: 'Don't go in there, Christy, we can't afford it!' Then she had to leg it to the other end of the street and down the quays, where she found him knocking on a window of the new trade union skyscraper, Liberty Hall. They wouldn't let him in because he didn't have a union card, so his mother, highly indignant now, told all and sundry that the Labour Party hadn't been the same since that threesome, Conor, Cruise and O'Brien had joined it ...

Christy was eventually rescued by his mother from the roof of the Rotunda Maternity Hospital, prompting the headline in the *Evening Mail*: TEN-STONE BOY DELIVERED IN THE ROTUNDA! MOTHER AND CHILD DOING WELL!

How things have changed for us and I suppose I will have to face up to it now. My Claim to Fame is gone; in the supermarket I was known as 'Maureen Potter's husband' and when people came up to me and asked 'How is she?' we all knew exactly what and whom they meant.

When she herself was asked, she invariably mentioned Parkinson's disease. I never took that short cut. I always said: 'The arthritis is not too good' and that got me over the dilemma.

After her death, I received a nice letter from her consultant in the Mater Hospital, who said she had a 'bad neurological problem that remained mysterious to the end'.

Long before that, I saw an ad in the chemist's shop about a meeting of the Parkinson's Society but we never got to it. Maybe we should have and it might have prepared me for her sudden passing.

I'm three years older than she was – and always told her that she was catching up on me. So one of these days she will.

JACK O'LEARY.

PART I

Entrance

What was most encouraging about gathering contributions for this book was the extraordinarily high percentage of immediate and unconditional agreement from, not only her former colleagues, but also a wide and eclectic cross-section of Maureen Potter's audience, even those most pressured by politics, business or work of all sorts.

'A-aahhhh, Maureen! Of course I'll do something.'

'I wouldn't be a great writer, but I'll have a go.'

'It'd be a privilege. Thank you for thinking of me.'

'I loved her. We all loved her.'

There are contradictions, of course: she was penniless as a child/she was middle-class and lived in a big house; she hated others to get laughs that were by right hers/she was most generous with the limelight, particularly to young people; she could have made millions if she had gone to America but she stayed at home out of loyalty/she wouldn't have made it if she'd gone to America because her humour was too local. Opinions divide along the lines of personal perspective. Memories differ too. For instance, was it 'Save your breath to cool your porridge' or 'Keep your breath to cool your porridge.' Does it matter?

This is not a biography but an homage from 100 friends, including Tommy the Theatre Cat, *Maureen's beloved Bobby, the feline she immortalised in the book she wrote for children.*

BERTIE AHERN

The first thing that I think about when I hear Maureen Potter's name is Christy.

When I was a child, Maureen Potter and her son, Christy, were a feature on the radio every Sunday at lunchtime in our house. Everyone in Ireland knows who Maureen was, but Christy is less well known now: he was an imaginary and not very bright son who was a constant source of disappointment to his long-suffering, if loving, mother. The sketches, listened to all over the country, were very funny; poor Christy never had much luck and I think that we found it so funny because there is a bit of the Christy in us all!

Maureen and Christy were a big part of our Sunday for

years – great entertainment (it is difficult now to imagine that there was a time when nearly everyone was at home on Sunday and the family lunch was a big event in the week).

My mother brought me regularly to Maureen's Pantos as well, a great treat for a child, so she was a big part of my growing up in Dublin.

In real life, I met her many times. She was a north-side Dub, very interested in community and local issues, and I found her to be a kind and generous lady.

A lot of her work has been recorded for posterity and I think that these classics of comedy and entertainment will give great pleasure for many years to come.

Maureen Potter was a real 'star' in the old meaning of the word.

On the night of 18 January 1999, Maureen Potter was honoured in the Gaiety Theatre by a succession of colleagues and admirers from all walks of life. It was a long evening and by the end of it people in the audience were tired. It was very hot and getting hotter: jackets, boleros and stoles had long been discarded, and although the quality of the entertainment and continuing tribute on stage was mighty, people had begun to look surreptitiously at their watches.

Then the little comedienne herself walked on stage for the final act, the

Souvenir programme from the
Maureen Potter tribute.
Courtesy of Abhann

presentation to her of her portrait, commissioned from the artist James Hanley; it was as if, communally, the audience had received a huge jolt of adrenaline because, as one, they shot instantly to their feet to give her a standing ovation.

On and on it went, for the best part of five or six minutes, as she stood, caught like a little owl in the spotlight.

JAMES HANLEY

Maureen with James Hanley. Courtesy of James Hanley

In the autumn of 1998 I was commissioned by John McColgan to paint a portrait of Maureen Potter to celebrate her association with the Gaiety Theatre.

Maureen insisted on coming to my studio, which is at the top of three flights of steep stairs on Trinity Street. As nearly everyone finds this staircase to be hard work, I thought it would be too much for her, a lady in her seventies, and so had offered to go to meet her in her own house. But she wanted to come to me. Maureen was physically a tiny woman, but even at that stage of her life, she had retained her characteristic look – bright eyes behind big glasses and her trademark hat.

Having a portrait painted can be a difficult process for

some people. Many sitters are uncomfortable with the focused attention and even people whose livelihoods depend on their physical appearance can feel awkward. Myself and Maureen discussed a variety of possible poses, but none really seemed right. When finally I asked her to strike a pose that felt natural to her, Maureen immediately took the curtain call, dramatic and appropriate, creating an ideally theatrical image.

Her husband, Jack, asked me why I wasn't painting her in her prime, making her younger than she was, but I paint people as they are, and I felt the portrait's impact and poignancy would lie in expressing Maureen's accumulated experience and the history which came as part of her.

Although she was so small in stature, I wanted her to dominate the canvas, so I painted her slightly larger than life-size. And I wanted to include the Gaiety in the painting, which created problems of juxtaposing a single small figure against a vast interior. To solve this problem, I showed the theatre reflected in a mirror behind her, making sense of her gesture to an imagined audience, making the viewer part of her audience in the theatre. The reflection in the mirror also meant that I could reduce the scale of the theatre, so including all the tiers of the Gaiety in its splendour.

Because Maureen was such a well-known national figure who had such a long and varied career, people have many different memories of her. I tried to do justice to this by including images and photos of some of her immediately recognisable roles – the dancing nun, the young Shirley Temple look-alike, in full flow with Danny Cummins, the usherette – and I propped them behind the mirror as they would be seen in any theatrical dressing room or over anyone's fireplace mantel.

My work as a portrait painter means I have the opportunity to meet some extraordinary people who have reached a point of success in their lives and their careers. They are each individually fascinating and invariably and unfailingly polite. Maureen fit that pattern exactly. She was warm and funny, and she treated me and what I had to do with absolute graciousness and generosity of time and spirit. She was interested in everything and full of chat. During her time in my studio, she told me stories of the North Strand, where my wife and I had recently bought our first home, of her own wedding in Fairview, stories of her early married life.

I asked her if she felt there was an expectation of her to be always in character or 'on' and if she found that a chore. She told me a funny story Tommy Cooper had told her about being invited to a dinner party where, once the meal was finished, guests were ushered into a room where chairs had been arranged in a semi-circle and where he was handed a deck of cards as he came in the door, expected to entertain, to sing for his supper. He used some colourful language, threw the cards up in the air and walked out …

Maureen Potter did a good Tommy Cooper.

The following January, the finished painting was unveiled on the stage of the Gaiety at the end of the gala celebration of Maureen's life and work. President McAleese performed the unveiling ceremony.

Maureen had seen it that evening in the green room. She had walked over to it and, dwarfed by its size, examined it carefully. Then: 'Warts and all,' she said and laughed. I thought she seemed so tiny and frail in appearance, but later that evening, when once again she got out there on that stage, her personality was immense.

We were brought to lunch some days later, when the painting was finally hung in its present location in the Gaiety. Maureen had thoroughly enjoyed the gala evening and was pleased with her portrait. She was delighted the President had been there to unveil it and was warm and appreciative about people's participation in the event.

We had spoken about many things at our initial meeting, including pets, and I had mentioned that my wife loved hounds, particularly lurchers. Ever the pro, never forgetting a thing, the last thing Maureen said to me as she was leaving that lunch was: 'Don't forget to get your wife that little dog!'

The playwright Hugh Leonard wrote a warm, loving piece in the souvenir programme for that night of tribute and celebrations, opining that he was pretty sure Shakespeare had Maureen Potter in mind when he wrote Twelfth Night.

It is my favourite play, and in idle moments I like to do the casting for a production which will one day be mounted in Elysium. Stan Laurel will play Sir Andrew Aguecheek, with Oliver Hardy as Sir Toby Belch. Charles Laughton will make the definitive Malvolio, and Potter will, of course, be Maria. And I shall commit unrepentant sacrilege by filching a line from Sir Toby and giving it to her, for in my mind's eye she is hopping on to a stool the better to come nose to nose with Laughton for 'Dost though think, because thou art virtuous, there shall be no more cakes and ale?' I can see and hear her, as plain as plain.

While I am about it, I would have her play the nurse in *Romeo and Juliet* and Mrs Malaprop in *The Rivals*. Then, if Dickens can be persuaded to adapt a few of his novels for the theatre – or I might do it for him! – she would make a glorious Peggoty, a scarifying Sairey Gamp and, choosing if she so wishes, since this is heaven, to turn herself into a younger Potter, a show-stopping Infant Prodigy.

Writing of Laurence Olivier and Vivien Leigh in *Antony and Cleopatra*, Kenneth Tynan said that 'Sir Laurence, with that curious chivalry which some time or other blights the progress of every great actor, gives me the impression that he blunts his blow-lamp ebullience to match her. Antony climbs down, and Cleopatra pats him on the head.' Reversing the sexes, there were times when the same could be said of Potter: that perhaps because O'Dea was, after all, the guv'nor, she met him a little more than half-way. When at last the long apprenticeship was over and she flew solo, there were great days. Unlike many a lesser comedian, she was content with causing our sides to split and our rib cages to ache; she did not aspire to break our hearts as well. Once Chaplin heard from his audience an 'Ah!' or an 'Aw!' of compassion, he was done for. He became Charles instead of Charlie – Potter had too much self-respect for pathos.

She had the gift (Tommy Cooper, too, comes to mind) of seeing herself with a cold eye. She knew exactly what she looked like in performance; it was not subjective, but the truth, and she played to it. To use an ungainly piece of imagery, no matter where you would choose to strike her, it would not yield a false note.

It is a cliché of show business that every comedian wants to play Hamlet. Potter did not – she played Maisie Madigan. (Pascal wrote that if Cleopatra's nose had been shorter the entire history of the world might have been different. One could say that if Maureen Potter had been three inches taller, the history of Irish theatre would have been gloomier.) Going 'legitimate' was an act of rare courage: not because anyone could for an instant doubt Potter's ability to inhabit another skin, but because by doing so she was severing the bond between herself and the audience. She was no longer Maureen Potter, playing directly to the faces across the 'foots', but, in the words of Captain Boyle, 'Mrs Madigan, an oul' back-parlour neighbour, who, if she could help it at all, would never see a body shook.'

Potter is a 110-per-center. She is the person I most respect and admire in the theatre. And, if that isn't enough, she is the biggest little woman I know.

∽

On Spy Wednesday, 2004, Maureen Potter made her entrance into Elysium. It was five years, two months, two weeks and three days after that night at the Gaiety. She was buried on Easter Saturday and the following day Hugh Leonard marked her passing as follows.

Picture, if you will, a rehearsal room high up under the eaves of the Abbey Theatre. Waiting for her next cue, a small woman – Maureen Potter – sits to one side of the acting area.

Now and again, she steals a look at the author of the play, *Moving*, whom she has not yet met.

She is shaking with nerves. She wonders if perhaps he is harbouring doubts about her. Is she – a vaudevillian since the year dot – fit to be entrusted with a 'straight' part? She is mistaken, for what is bothering him is not her unworthiness, but his. Is she asking herself if her role and the play itself are good enough? And he is remembering how, although Mo Potter and he are only a few years apart in age, his parents somehow scraped the money together every year to take him to the Gaiety Theatre to see what Dickens would have called an Infant Prodigy.

So there they are, the pair of them: he waiting for her to walk out on the play and him, she waiting to be walked out on. The rehearsal continues on its course, with actor and author, both excruciatingly shy, squaring off at each other like fighters waiting for the starting bell. After a particular scene, she returns to her chair, and the author whispers to the director, one Joe Dowling: 'Potter is bloody marvellous.' Joe says: 'Well, for God's sake go over and tell her so ... She's in bits, thinking you don't like her.'

So I did as I was told. I went over and said: 'Excuse me, Miss Potter, but I think you're bloody marvellous.' And, of course, there and then she burst into tears.

I saw the other side of her a couple of weeks later, when the portrait of a certain playwright was being unveiled in the Abbey bar. Unexpectedly, after the speeches had been made, the subject of the painting declared that he wanted to contribute a homily of his own and launched into a filibuster. As he guffed on, Potter came over to me and whispered a dirty limerick into my ear.

As if this were not enough, she then sang a little song to me; it was even bawdier than the limerick and had to do with two sticks: a cleft and a bent one. Naturally, I let loose a yelp of hysteria, and as the speechifying playwright glared – and indeed he has not spoken to me since – Mo Potter turned her eyes skywards and contrived to look as if she had but lately come down to earth with a flight of angels.

That was in 1991, but my first sighting of her was as an eleven-year-old boy in the Gaiety. The setting of a certain comic sketch was a village shop; Jimmy O'Dea was the shopkeeper and Potter entered as a customer. She wore curlers that were all too visible under a floral head-scarf, a grey cardy that was out at the elbows and wellington boots that all but came up to her chin. Her first line was 'Me fayther [father] wants to know if you have anything for a bile [boil] on a bull' (anything a salacious mind cares to imagine).

Maureen with Barnard Hughes and Donal McCann in Da.
Courtesy of Jack O'Leary

Years – many years – passed, and I caught my first off-stage sighting of her at close range in 1989 when, with eight other Dubliners, she and I were conferred with doctorates by TCD. As we stood in line and shuffled forward to receive the accolade, or the native version of same, Mo was sandwiched between Gay Byrne and me. Mr Byrne and I were po-faced, as befitted the occasion – in fact there were cries of 'Howya, Gay?' from the on-looking polloi to which he gravely replied to his fans with 'Good day to you' – but Mo Potter simply stuck her tongue out at the cameras.

After *Moving*, in which she was indeed 'bloody marvellous', my wife, Paule, and I became friends with her and her husband, Jack O'Leary. Probably she knew everyone in 'the business', and her inclusion of me as what she would call an 'old segotia' was – to myself at any rate – inexplicable. However, as a director friend of mine said when we received a good review, but for a nonsensical reason, one does not argue with Yes.

Mo was generous – astonishingly so in a profession in which hard times often breed a steeliness to match. And she was riotously, absurdly funny. Comics rarely are; off-stage, her long-time partner, Jimmy O'Dea, was one of the most mournful persons one could meet.

She could sing and dance, but I think her greatest gift was for creating laughter, whether as a farceuse, as a comic genius with a gift for parody or, simply, as a star of pantomime.

I did a foolish thing where Potter was concerned, and it had to do with a forty-five minute play, *The Lily Lally Show*. It was a play for one actress, or one actor, as we say nowadays in an attempt to appease the feminist hordes. There are those who believe that the play was an attempt on my part to portray Mo herself. It was nothing of the kind; it tried to bring to life a kind of comedy – no, of theatre – that was dying piecemeal with the passing of O'Dea, Cruise, Cummins, Sheridan and now Potter herself. She was the greatest of them, not because she survived, but because she had a spirit as mighty as her physical height was small.

She should have played in *The Lily Lally Show*, but at her age we thought that she would have had trouble learning the lines. The part went to Barbara Brennan, who was superb and all that an author could desire, but somehow in a deep sense the play belonged to Potter.

This week she entered into legend. Like spendthrifts, we have used up all the superlatives, and how often have we heard that a loved player was the greatest, the most iconic, the most irreplaceable, unforgettable, exceptional. The thesaurus has been emptied, and it is no matter, for words are not enough. Our hearts are scalded.

I coined a line in that play of mine, *Moving*, and – out of arrogance, perhaps – let me use it here. She was the bestest.

(First printed in the *Sunday Independent* on Easter Sunday, 11 April 2004. Reprinted by kind permission of the author.)

BARBARA BRENNAN

Maureen with Barbara Brennan and Des Smyth in *Dick Whittington* at the Gaiety. Photo: James D. O'Callaghan

Along with many others, my first glimpse of Maureen Potter was in Pantomime when I was a child – I thought she was fascinating and, of course, funny – herself and Jimmy O'Dea made Christmas for us for many years.

Later, I remember going along on Sunday afternoons to the O'Connell Hall to watch radio recordings of *The Maureen Potter Show*, produced by Fred O'Donovan. This also starred my late father, Denis Brennan, which, of course, is why we were there. They did a sketch together every week called *Jim and Agnes* – the ending of which always went:

She: 'Oh Jem –?'

He: 'Yis Ag-eniss –?'

Then there was a pregnant pause, during which every radio listener in the land took a deep breath, ready to roar along with her and:

She: 'Rip it up Jem! Rip it up!'

Incidentally this radio show also featured Eugene Lambert with his puppet, Finnegan, and was probably one of the very few ventriloquist acts to be heard on radio anywhere. (Of course, this was an era where, on the same Radio Éireann, the Rory O'Connor Dancers were to be heard rattling up a storm every week for their host, Din Joe.)

When I was sixteen, Alice Dalgarno came to our ballet school to audition dancers for the Gaiety Pantomime and I was offered one of the jobs. I couldn't believe it – I was now going to be a part of this show that had meant so much to me in my childhood; going to be on the same stage as this woman who filled me with awe.

We rehearsed the dancing with Alice in the Television Club at the top of Harcourt Street, then came down to the theatre to join the cast for the last week; and when we walked into what used to be called the Tea Lounge, Maureen Potter came over to greet us. There was no Them and Us, it seemed; we were all in this together. Having said that, however, the dancers usually kept to their side of the stage and the Principals to theirs.

That first pantomime was *Robin Hood* and it had a very long and successful run; so much so that on the last night the junior members of the cast were in floods of tears at the finale – thinking that they would never have this wonderful experience again. Little did I know that this was to be the first of eight Pantos I was to do with Maureen, two as a dancer, one as an Ingénue and five as Principal Girl. To my delight, I was also asked to perform in her summer shows, *Gaels of Laughter*.

To be given the opportunity to observe Maureen's talent, vivacity and perfectionism (whether she was singing 'Send in the Clowns' from the top of a ladder at the opening of *Gaels*, dancing a tap and Irish dancing routine with the Irish champion Brian O'Connor, performing 'The Angels on the O'Connell Monument' sketch with Danny Cummins in Panto or her own solo acts and political fairytales written by her husband, Jack O'Leary), and at such close quarters, was a rare privilege.

As an aside, there were some hairy moments with the specialty acts, especially in Panto and especially involving animals. One I particularly remember involved some very unruly seals and disobedient penguins. One of the seals got away from the trainer and flopped onto the stage in the middle of the sketch; 'Oh look –' said Danny Cummins, always quick as a whip with the ad libs, 'the Liffey is risin'!'

Maureen was always in top form, consistently at her glittering and hilarious best. Whatever ills she might have had off-stage – laryngitis, bad knees – her love for her audience and her craft made her leave her woes in the wings and Doctor Theatre carried her on stage to weave her spell and enthral those people out front.

And what a loyal audience she did have – her relationship with them was unparalleled because she appealed to everyone, from five-year-olds to octogenarians.

She made it look easy, but she sure didn't think so, pacing up and down outside the Number One dressing room in the Gaiety before every first night, more nervous than anybody. As she stood in the wings before she went on, waiting to go from the dark to the light, she was like a coiled spring, but when she hit that stage to thunderous applause, the nerves disappeared and the laughter started.

Her comedy didn't come just from funny lines, though

these were all delivered to perfection and with brilliant timing. Her dancing was funny (as in the 'Come Dancing' sketch with Danny Cummins; not a word spoken but hilarious from beginning to end; also the wonderful extempore and eccentric dance she did to drum accompaniment, first from Joe Bonnie, then George Reilly and finally Desi Reynolds, making it almost a competition to see if she could catch them out ...)

I moved on from the Gaiety in the mid-1970s and after that my meetings with Maureen were only occasional.

I remember meeting her once in the dance centre in Litton Lane – she was rehearsing *Da* by Hugh Leonard for the Olympia; I was rehearsing something else – and she confided in me that she was sick with nerves about it. 'Nonsense. Of course you'll be wonderful,' said I, but I could see by her reaction that how she felt and how others felt about her were two totally different things.

Maureen and the cast of *Dick Whittington* at the Gaiety.
Photo: James D. O'Callaghan

In 1994, I was asked to play the character, Mary Moone, in the one-woman play *The Lily Lally Show*, also written by Leonard. Scheduled as the second play of two at the Abbey Theatre and directed by Patrick Mason, it was clear from the start that the play owed much to the existence of Maureen Potter, as Hugh Leonard himself acknowledged in his obituary of her in the *Sunday Independent*. Although it wasn't deliberately biographical, if you were going to give a play about an Irish comedienne, there was only one.

The sections that to me show the true Maureen are when we see Mary Moone doing her stand-up act. Where before had I seen that grit and determination, that rapport with an audience? It is a great piece, written in homage to a unique performer, and on the opening night an enormous basket of flowers was delivered to my dressing room. It was from Maureen herself, who was Hugh Leonard's guest of honour that night.

When they came back afterwards, she put her arms around me. 'When you said Tangier Lane,' she said with tears in her eyes, 'I could smell it!' (Tangier Lane is where the stage door of the Gaiety and the back door of Neary's pub are situated; the back entrance to Sawyer's fish shop is there too, so the smell is quite pungent!) This was Maureen at her most generous and understanding, because I'm sure she knew I would feel trepidation knowing she was in the audience that night. And it didn't end there. She stood by me all that night in the Abbey bar, truly a great support.

On another occasion, when she and I were both guests at an opening of another Leonard play, *Love in the Title*, she told me she'd love to go backstage to meet the three actresses in the show, so I said I would take her. She took my arm and we tried to edge our way across the thronged first-night Abbey bar. Of course, it took forever because everyone wanted to say 'hello' to her or to simply chat.

When we did eventually get backstage to the dressing room and I opened the door to announce her, the looks of shock on the faces of the three – Ingrid Craigie, Catherine Walsh and Karen Ardiff – had to be seen to be believed.

Maureen's eyes welled up again – she could be very emotional – as she told them all how great she thought they were, with that generosity of spirit and genuine love of those who had gone out there and delivered.

Maureen Potter evoked great and passionate feelings of love in everyone who came near her, love of performance, of theatre, of audiences; of joy in performing, of consistency in every performance – never a mistake, never a drop in energy.

What an icon for those of us who were lucky enough to have the chance to work alongside her!

I'll miss her, but I'll never, ever forget her.

JOHN O'DONOGHUE, T.D.

Maureen Potter was an artist of many talents, but to me by far the most significant one was her ability to make an entire nation laugh.

As a nation, we have always excelled in private wit. When Maureen Potter was at the height of her powers we were, perhaps, less effective at public humour. She helped us discover the value of laughing at and with each other.

For more than two generations, Maureen delighted audiences with her distinctive brand of humour and sense of fun. Maureen was a beacon of light that added much-needed gaiety to the nation, no matter how bad things seemed.

Her favourite targets were the powers-that-be. At a time when people were far more respectful to those in authority than they are today, she spared nobody in puncturing the pretentious and poking fun at those who sought to get above themselves. In doing so, she became a national institution herself, but one that was universally loved. Even those who were on the receiving end of her humour loved her, because they recognised that its gentle touch meant no harm.

For very many people in Ireland today, enjoying a show with Maureen Potter was an integral part of childhood – an enjoyment that extended into adult life and is now an unforgettable memory.

At the mention of Maureen Potter's name, people smile as memories of magical childhood visits to the Gaiety Theatre in Dublin return to life.

I was one of those children who was lucky enough to experience these outings and so the memory of Maureen Potter on stage encompasses much of my youth. It was not just the fact that she was small in stature that endeared her to us children but also her talent in being able to communicate so naturally.

To this day I cannot pass the O'Connell monument in O'Connell Street in Dublin without thinking of the wonderful sketch where the curtain opened and there were Maureen Potter and Danny Cummins, dressed as two of the angels on that statue, giving a hilarious running commentary on the goings-on in O'Connell Street. The antics of Maureen Potter and 'her Christy' were enjoyed by many a generation.

It was certainly not uncommon for adults to bring along children to Maureen's performances just to have the excuse to be there themselves!

Jimmy O'Dea and Maureen as O'Connell Street angels.
Courtesy of the Sunday Independent

My father, Terry, remembers seeing one of Maureen's very first performances in the Gaiety in the early 1930s, when she would have been about nine years of age. She was playing the accordion and was with the great Jimmy O'Dea.

As I grew older, I began to appreciate the political sketches, which were always very clever. While the performances poked fun at her victims, she was never wounding or cruel. It was her genuinely mischievous personality that ignited the very effective interplay between herself and her audience.

Maureen Potter was also a very respected serious actor, but for me she will always be that very special comedian.

In later years we were to learn of the great physical pain she suffered, but, typical of Maureen, her audience would never have guessed. She very successfully mastered the pain with her professionalism and a great sense of fun.

When Maureen Potter died, a part of the childhood in us died with her.

LIZ McMANUS, T.D.

As a child I had my doubts about Jimmy O'Dea. All that make-up and women's clothing spooked me.

Maureen Potter was a different story. She passed herself off as an adult and yet we children knew, secretly, that she was one of us; a bundle of mischief whizzing around the Gaiety stage through gales of laughter and gasps of wonder.

Each year my father said he brought us girls to the Christmas Panto as a family treat. He was fooling nobody. He went to enjoy himself and sat roaring with laughter as loudly as any four-year-old.

On Radio Éireann, Christy's mammy recounted her trials and tribulations. We never heard what Christy had to say for himself, but his hangdog presence was as real to us as if he had a speaking part in the saga. Mammy brought tears of laughter to our eyes but, in our hearts, we identified with poor, accident-prone Christy. It was Christy after all, on one glorious occasion, who ended up being carried over the rooftops of O'Connell Street, clutching a bunch of Bradley's Shoe Shop balloons.

Years later I saw Maureen Potter in *Juno and the Paycock*, performing with great actors like Donal McCann and John Kavanagh. She skitted around the stage, full of the old energy and verve.

Years later again, I saw a television programme about her and discovered that, at the time, she was crippled with arthritis. Yet there she was dancing like a child around the kitchen in the O'Casey play. A true trooper, Maureen Potter had great courage, great talent and a great heart. She will be long remembered.

Maureen and Jimmy O'Dea (Mrs Mulligan and daughter).
Courtesy of Abhann

What one remembers over a long period of time seems arbitrary and inexplicable. Why should I have a clear recall of Maureen Potter in a Pantomime over forty years ago, when my recollection of important pieces of business three decades later is hazy and imprecise?

I don't recall going to the Pantomime, but being at it. I recall nothing of the actors other than Maureen Potter. I was too young to register her diminutive stature, but registered unerringly that she was the star of the show. Her immense energy, constant presence on stage, near-constant movement and distinctive carrying voice left no doubt of that.

The world of the early sixties, the Ban-the-Bomb marches in England, the first stirrings of modernity here, is recalled in a verse of one of her kindly satirical songs which, extraordinarily, has lingered in my memory after so long:

In London and England the crowds are all out
For banning the bomb and its awful fall out
But our GAA have a much better plan
For some of the club propose Bombing the Ban.

About the same time, Maureen had a radio programme which, as I recall, went out on Sundays. The main character was a Liberties mother driven to distraction by her son Christy – 'C'mon Christy,' shouted in broad Dublinese, supplying the start of each monologue. All Christy's fingers were thumbs and he and his mother got into countless scrapes, which the mother character would explain in her invariable closing: 'Honestly, we're just unfortunate.' These sketches were eagerly talked about on the bus to school by the very last pre-TV generation.

Maureen exuded the romance of the theatre, but she was so local in her references, so rooted in the Dublin of those days, that she was much more of a real individual to her audience than a mere actress could have been. Though she lived in the glamour of grease paint and limelight, which she exploited so well, this rootedness gave her gentle humour the intimate quality of family banter. That, I think, is why she has lived so long and so happily in the memory of those for whom she performed in their childhood.

Maureen, in Shakespeare's phrase, was 'such stuff as dreams are made of'. But unlike the actors Shakespeare described, her theatrical life was no 'insubstantial pageant'. It was part and parcel of a Dublin childhood and of the happiest, most eagerly recalled moments of it.

JOHN BRUTON

Maureen Potter was, above all, a Dublin comedian. She captured the mild mockery of oneself and of others that characterised Dublin wit. I remember Maureen and Jimmy O'Dea in Pantomime and also Mícheál MacLíammóir.

JOHN DUNNE

Years ago
I used to crow
'Hurray! Hurray!'
It's Potter Day!

Children raring –
Adults sharing
Sweeties, ices
Chocs, surprises.

Christy soaring
His ma roaring,
Barons, princes,
Giant mincers.

Blameless fun,
Scoundrels 'done',
Lives enriched
With mammoth gifts.

All the talents
All the skills
For Pantos, plays,
For run-of-the-mills.

Extraordinaire
A breath of air
And now she's gone
The love lives on.

TONY O'REILLY

Maureen Potter was, quite simply, part of my childhood. A mysterious, selectively remembered past, in which mainly the good things are recalled. My mother, whom I adored, took me regularly to the old Theatre Royal – to my eyes, a vast roman amphitheatre populated by leggy dancers and by three central stars: Noel Purcell, Jimmy O'Dea and the unsinkable Maureen Potter.

She mixed the gamine and the imperious in a way that was hugely funny to my young eyes. The Christmas Pantomime with the cry, when the evil Baron appeared to her Goldilocks, 'Look out behind you,' will remain an abiding memory.

She made Dublin a magical place to grow up in. With all that the city offers today, no one can replace her.

TREVOR SARGENT, T.D.

My memories of Maureen have been shared over the years with mother and father, brother and sister, when we reminisce about attending the Pantomime, where the larger-than-life presence of Maureen Potter, Jack Cruise, Mr Curran and others gave us the best-value entertainment money could buy – and pains in our sides from laughing.

Those joys in themselves would be impressive tributes to any thespian, but in the case of Maureen Potter, she also had the air of a magician about her, as it was hard to figure out how she remembered the names of all the boys and girls who had birthdays, etc., and needed to be mentioned for one reason or another.

In the intervening years, it has occurred to me that she must have had a superhuman memory – which should not come as any surprise, as so many of her great qualities were superhuman in anybody's book.

MAEVE BINCHY

You'd never think that they'd worry about filling the Gaiety for Maureen Potter, but it seems they did.

We would come in on the bus to see the Pantomime every Christmas and, at the end, there would be little Maureen stood on the stage, dressed like an elf or a Tom Thumb or a Dick Whittington, urging us to tell our friends if we liked it. It didn't seem at all necessary; the place was full to the rafters anyway. But we always spread the word for Maureen because she had asked us boys and girls to do it.

And, like any business, the company must have had commercial anxieties, so from time to time they would seek a little publicity by inviting a journalist in to do an interview or watch a rehearsal.

Over the years working in *The Irish Times*, I was sent out on some lovely jobs and some really awful jobs, but I think the day in the early 1970s when I was sent to write about Maureen Potter was one of the best.

I was smiling all the way up Grafton Street, thinking how lucky I was and how every small child – and, indeed, every big child – in the country would envy me going in there for an hour to see how the magic of pantomime came together.

This star was so far from being 'starry' you wouldn't believe it – wearing glasses and a knitted hat and darting about a lot like a tiny, busy, over-active aunt. If someone had told you she had come in with someone's packed lunch you'd have thought that was quite reasonable.

She was very, *very* small.

I am very big.

And so I spent the first ten minutes of the encounter moving backwards and sideways trying not to step on her.

After a bit, she realised that I seemed to be moving all the time and asked me if anything was wrong. I told her truthfully that I didn't want to crush her and so destroy Christmas for a whole generation.

She was very practical about it. People were always in danger of standing on her, she said; so she had learned to take evasive action early on and nowadays was nifty at avoiding bruising encounters.

And then it came to rehearsing *her* bit.

And she was transformed.

There was no audience there that day apart from myself and the company, but you would have sworn she had an audience of thousands out there the way she delivered the script and danced and gave her whole little body and her huge heart to the performance.

Pencil and notebook on my lap, I sat there, star struck.

When her bit was over, the subject of my interview had to remind me that I was meant to be taking notes and, hurriedly, I took a few so I could write a piece to help take the bare look off the place when the show opened.

I met her many times after that and saw that, like a tiny epicentre of goodwill, wherever she went she spread cheer in all directions. For instance, with her incredible recall, she always knew everyone's name.

I last met her at Billie Barry's retirement party, where we sat and discussed arthritis with the animated, ghoulish cheer that only those who have had new hips can muster. She said then that we sounded like a pair of auld ones and that the next time we met we should talk about sex from the outset.

I was always looking forward to that conversation which, sadly, will now not take place in this life.

Maureen with Maeve Binchy and Billie Barry.
Courtesy of Billie Barry

Little Mo.

Maureen Potter. Little Mo to us, big Mo being Maureen Toal.

As children Maureen and I lived a few doors from each other in Philipsburgh Avenue, Fairview. I played with her brothers but Maureen was rarely about. She was abroad much of the time, already working professionally and well on the way to becoming the star she was born to be.

It was in Neary's Bar in the 1950's that we got to know each other over 'the odd inoffensive jar' in company with Jimmy O'Dea and Myles na Gopaleen. She it was who suggested to Jimmy that we would work well together and so it was thanks to Mo that I became Jimmy's partner in a much loved TV series by Myles. Several revues and pantos at the Gaiety followed. Anything I know about comedy I learned then.

Later I played in two 'Gaels of Laughter' and two pantos with her when pay day became her cue to spend what must have been most of her salary on gifts for everyone. I still have some silk ties from Tysons of Grafton Street which I wear with pride for good reason.

Our last appearance together was in a Chekov play at the Gate Theatre. She was in great pain. The ill health that was to be her burden for the rest of her life had already started but each performance was a gem, a robust and energetic masterclass in style and indeed bravery.

Small in stature, little Mo was a giant.

Dana Kelly.

Ireland, as we all know, is an extended village and it is rare to go to any party, attend any gathering, without meeting someone who knows someone you know or, quite frequently, is somehow tenuously related to you by blood or marriage. In the context of a book about Maureen Potter, it was therefore perhaps not too surprising to find that the former Taoiseach, Charles J. Haughey, has a family connection to Potter via Jimmy O'Dea.

Jimmy O'Dea's brother, Laurence, who was also an actor – stage name Lionel Day – married Maureen Haughey's maternal aunt, Gertie Hughes, and so became her uncle-in-law. O'Dea himself was best man to her father, former Taoiseach Seán Lemass. So, as a family, the Haugheys always maintained a proprietorial interest in the goings-on at the Gaiety and, of course, attended the Pantomimes there.

As a result, in tribute to Maureen Potter and as a 'thank you' for the hours of simple happiness and hilarity they experienced in the comfortable darkness of the auditorium, they were happy to lend these photographs.

Maureen and Charles J. Haughey. Courtesy of Charles J. Haughey

Jimmy O'Dea with Seán Lemass and his wife Kathleen.
Courtesy of Charles J. Haughey

Mr Haughey himself refers to Potter's gift – 'the compelling ability to make us all laugh, no matter how dismal the world around us might seem' – as 'priceless'. And like most, he too remembers with amazement her facility for the faultless recall of a long list of names, including the names of his own children; these may have lived in a mansion and become accustomed to being well known in their own worlds, but they were as thrilled as any other kid in that audience on hearing themselves mentioned. 'The fact that they were included among thirty or more equally ardent young fans made not the slightest difference.'

The Haugheys frequently brought along some of the kids' friends to the Panto as well and, according to Maureen Haughey, when reciting her 'litany' at the end, Potter always made a substantial meal from the name of one of them.

While the Haughey row trembled in anticipation, with one little hand clamped as an eye-shade to her forehead, the comedienne would first survey the audience in wide, exaggerated sweeps, right to left of the orchestra pit and back again. 'Where is he?'

Sweeping around the boxes. 'Where is he?'

Then, top to bottom, gods to parterre and back up again:
'Where's that Magoo Murnane?'

Oh, ecstasy!

⌒

DEIRDRE PURCELL

Mo Po's first public appearance was not on a stage but in a
courtroom. She was a pupil of the Connie Ryan Dancing
School in Abbey Street, above Buckley's shop, the proprietor
of which objected strongly to the incessant thundering above
the heads of himself and his customers. Naturally he
complained, frequently, and when the complaints did not
bear fruit, he took the school to court.

Miss Ryan brought the tiny Maureen Potter into the court
with her as evidence for the defence. While she hummed and
la-la'd the tune, little Mo danced a reel around the courtroom
on fairy feet.

The judge dismissed the case. *Noise? What noise?*

There was never a career other than show business in
prospect for Maria Philomena Potter, so christened because,

A young Maureen Potter. Courtesy of Jack O'Leary

in 1925, the baptising priest in Fairview, Dublin, would not accept 'Maureen' as a suitable name for a nice Catholic child. At an early, very early, age, she knew her own mind and how to exercise her will. For instance, she would attend the national school beside her house on Philipsburgh Avenue, St Mary's, only after the extraction of a promise that she would be allowed take lessons at the CYMS hall in the afternoons with the local dancing teacher, Dewey Byrne. This teacher, recognising talent when she saw it, swiftly passed her pupil on to Connie Ryan, who, with her brother, Michael, ran a much more sophisticated operation, including the training of the O'Dea girls – the chorus line for Jimmy O'Dea at the Theatre Royal.

In 'real' school, however, little Mo kept a low profile: 'She was quick and smart, but shy and very nervous. I thought she was sort of odd. She was liked, though, and never created trouble –' this from Mamie Browne (now Eakins) whose family ran a hairdressing salon, Maison Prost, and who shared a desk with her. 'She was great at the reading and the two of us were always picked to read to the class. I remember us reading *A Tale of Two Cities* but at that stage, I have to say, I saw no sign of any comic talent. Although, when our cat had three kittens, she insisted on us calling them Larry, Curly and Mo. She adored animals. Particularly cats.'

According to her friend, Maureen was a permanent clock-watcher at school, 'waiting for the big hand to get to the six after the two so she could run out and go to her dancing class, or later on she had to get to the matinée in the Theatre Royal. There must have been something in the air around Fairview. Dolly Sparks. She was a Royalette.'

Since, like Maureen, Mamie Browne had only brothers, the two became childhood surrogate sisters, always in and out of one another's homes, playing 'house' in back gardens, going to the pictures, playing tennis in The Crescent or picnicking on Dollymount Strand with other pals – but the littlest one never deviated from the grand plan to become a performer. Nothing was more important. 'She'd spend hours practising her dancing in front of a mirror at home. And when she was dancing at a *feis*, I'd notice that if she made a mistake, she simply stopped and started again. Her concentration was absolute. You got the impression that while she was dancing she lived in a world of her own.'

The personal training and preparation continued into the social life of the area. In the evenings, that particular coastal strip of Dublin, Fairview, Clontarf, Dollymount rang with piano music and song: 'There were all these great parties in everyone's houses. Her mother was a great pianist and singer, and in our house on Ballybough Road a Mr Crean, who was a music teacher in Artane School, would come and play the piano to accompany the party pieces and Maureen's dancing.'

The comedienne's father died when she was only seven years old, leaving her mother to rear her and her two brothers, Bob and Jimmy, without benefit of pension or even an insurance policy, yet she never expressed any sense or recollection of being poor. Perhaps it was because she was so busy winning chestfuls of medals in Irish dancing competitions. (At one point, having become Junior Dance Champion of Ireland, she pawned the medals and, far from handing over the spoils, treated herself and her cousin to chicken and chips in the Green Rooster restaurant on O'Connell Street.)

On the other hand, Mamie Browne remembers the constant sock washing that went on in the Potter household. 'She'd be going in and out to the Theatre Royal and the mother would wash the socks every night. Those were days when if you had three pairs of socks you were rich.'

The transition to the professional stage was early and swift. As one of Connie Ryan's Cute Kiddies, she was appearing as part of the stage show in the Star Cinema in Bray when Jimmy O'Dea, at the urging of Ryan, came to see her. As a result, he hired her to play the fairy guarding the beanstalk in his Pantomime *Jack and the Beanstalk* – and since productivity was a prerequisite for performers, he had a miniature morning suit made for her so that as Alfie Byrne, the then Lord Mayor of Dublin, she could also work a sketch with him.

Other Pantos (and variety and *feiseanna*) followed, so that by the age of twelve Maureen Potter was a seasoned pro and, billed now as a 'child impressionist and burlesque dancer', she left school to go on the road for the following two years with the bandleader and impresario Jack Hylton. 'We lent her a suitcase,' says Mamie Browne, 'and we did her hair. But her mother was very stressed about it.'

It was 1937 and, after the tours of England, one of the other countries to be toured was Germany.

Her adventures with Hitler and Goebbels are well documented and covered elsewhere by contributors to this book but while in Germany, wearing full Shirley Temple regalia, curly hair, fur coat and thigh-high gaiters made from white kid, she was taken to visit Berlin Zoo. 'I was a plain child,' she said in interview for the *Sunday Tribune* in the mid-eighties. 'Very plain. And they would insist on dressing me in these Shirley Temple clothes. Then people really did think that I was a dwarf, with thick black eyebrows and a scowl to match, under these hats with ribbons hanging down me back.' As a result, she swore that when she got back to Ireland she would never, ever curl her hair again, wear white kid or fur coats or gaiters. She threw the gaiters in the bin and for decades wore her hair severely straight and short.

She did come back to Ireland, much to her mother's relief, as war was about to break out. Straight away, however, she went on the road again, this time with her old mentor and in time, although still in her teens, graduated from being a soubrette – a singing, dancing ingénue – to the more satisfying role of straight 'feed' to Jimmy O'Dea. 'I was lucky,' she said. 'People who have been child stars usually don't make the transition. I grew with my profession.'

Pre-war touring with Hylton had been relatively plush, especially in England, where theatrical landladies ran impeccable establishments divided into 'combined chats' – bed-sittingrooms with separate sleeping and dining facilities – and vied with one another to cosset 'their' stars. 'When you got back from the theatre at night the fire in your room would be lit and your nice little supper all laid out on your table.'

Things were different back home. Professionally the company was every bit as competent as its UK counterpart. 'But, oh, the facilities!'

They travelled by lorry, except for James A. himself, who took advantage of his managerial status to travel ahead by car. The lorry carrying the rest of them would stop a quarter of a mile from the intended venue and the strolling players would dismount to brush off all the dust. And to live up to their Shakespearian titles, 'We would take the smaller of our suitcases and walk into town.' Nonchalantly, as if they had just got off a train. The 'baggage lorry', they announced grandly, was following with the gear.

Once in town, there was a scramble: first to find digs, then, in the hall, to bag a wall.

The wall was essential. Everyone carried a rope and two hooks. You screwed the hooks into the wall, if you found a free one, and the rope became your hanging wardrobe. If you could not find a wall, then you pinned your rope onto the permanent backdrop at the back of the stage.

As for the digs, they were appalling, with damp beds and damp sheets, overlaid with musty cretonne bedspreads. The allocation of water for washing each morning was usually half a pint of water per player.

They did look forward to the Belfast trips, however, because for these they travelled regally by train and got to know the crews. So when the train pulled in to Central Station, they were allowed stay on board while the carriages were rolled to The Beeches, about a mile back along the line. There they had a grand few jars, with a final 'one for the rails' before trailing back into the station.

O'Dea was careful to keep his young co-star's mother in the loop and paid frequent Sunday-morning visits to the house on Philipsburgh Avenue. 'He liked her,' Potter said, 'because she reminded him of his own little mother, always poking the fire and cleaning up around it. At that time the worst thing anyone could say about anybody else was: "That crowd was never used to a good fire!"'

During each of these visits, Mrs Potter would apparently look up from the tidying and the little bit of cleaning and the plumping and the poking to address her eminent guest: "'Now Mr O'Dea, won't you look after Maureen?"

"'I will, Mrs Potter. Don't you worry about Maureen,'" and, satisfied, Mrs Potter would return to her housewifely tasks.

'If only she knew!' Maureen herself laughed long and hard about this. 'I spent my life looking after him. I put him to bed, I woke him up. I remember one night, after a party, we all decided to sew up his pyjamas so he couldn't get into them. And you know who was left to unpick them and put him into them –'

So she played with him on stage and packed his bags for him on tour and learned and grew and fed him lines until he died. (Actually, there was something about her and packing bags. Because when John Ford worked with them both in the film *The Rising of the Moon*, he too 'allowed' her to pack his American military kit bag. 'He was sitting up there drinking his coffee and I was busy packing the bag for him.')

Jimmy O'Dea, Maureen and John Ford, on location in Kilkee for The Rising of the Moon, 1957. Courtesy of Jack O'Leary

By all accounts, including hers, O'Dea was sartorially a very meticulous little man, always beautifully dressed in handmade shirts from Tyson's and hand-sewn shoes. 'And he loved the Lord. [Lord Gormanston, the Hon. Patrick Campbell, etc.] But if some unfortunate ordinary Joe Soap put his head around the green room door, it was "Get out of this room! This is an artiste's room!"'

She laughed about this too, but affectionately. Her loyalty to him never wavered.

Although no one has claimed to know 'the real Maureen', gleaming through the stories in this volume are several strands that lit Maureen Potter's personality. For instance, her deeply ingrained sense of loyalty was not confined to those in the business: she continued to patronise Maison Prost right through to motherhood, when she would bring her two sons there to have their hair cut.

And while on stage she was generous with audiences and with the handing down of the tricks of the trade to young performers, off it she was just as big-hearted. George McFall, stage manager at the Gaiety Theatre for decades, reveals that there was a constant procession asking to see her. 'The number of people that came to the stage door asking for Maureen and she'd hand them out money; people never knew she did it, but I did. And she'd never pass a down-and-out artist in the street.

'She had a dresser called Annie long ago and poor Annie was skint; it was the only job she got, the Panto and then the summer show. Every weekend when Maureen'd get her weekend dinner – she got it in Buckley's of Chatham Street – she'd send around for it, and she always bought Annie's weekend meal as well. She was really kind like that.'

As for charity gigs, the stand-up comedian Hal Roach says that 'Never, ever, did she say "no" when I asked her.'

Her physical toughness and will-power – the triumph of will over serious pain and disability as soon as she hit the boards – remain legendary; her love of sports, particularly cricket, her genuine interest in the careers of others, her wide and eclectic reading patterns, her passion for current affairs, all get an airing.

This is not to say, however, that Maureen Potter has been

canonised. No performer gets to the top of a profession and stays there for so long without creating some ripples and there is a sub-text running under many of the pieces noting the harder side of this one's single-minded determination and drive.

George McFall says Potter could 'reef you' if a prop wasn't in its pre-assigned and rehearsed spot on the props table when she went to fetch it. 'It'd be a simple thing, she'd come screaming mad off the stage. You'd know with the Number One dressing-room door getting a bang.'

All who worked with her agree that she got over these minor explosions pretty quickly. 'You'd leave her alone for a few minutes,' says McFall, 'and then she'd come out: "I'm sorry".'

And on the last night of the run of each show, McFall would be given a fistful of envelopes, on each of which was written the name of every staff member in the theatre: 'Every single one. By name. To have a drink.'

Each of these professionals, all of whom miss her terribly and believe they will never see her likes again, smile with huge, reminiscent affection every time they say her name. Perfect consensus. There's no one like Maureen. Others try, but there'll never be another one.

In any interview she gave throughout her life, her own recollections about the main players in her stories were equally loving, with one or two exceptions. Never particularly religious in the strict observance of custom and practice, she was, as everyone acknowledges, Christian in the matter of 'doing unto others'. Charity deserted her, however, when it came to two subjects: cruelty to animals and Irish referendums, about both of which she became positively venomous. Not only about the generalities, but about people, particularly clerics, who attend – or who do not condemn – blood sports and who lecture about the moral conduct of ordinary folk.

That eighties *Sunday Tribune* interview had been conducted over a pleasant, very long lunch in Clontarf Castle, where the talk had meandered happily across the nostalgic territory of her past. But at the mention of religion, the tone changed abruptly. She sat bolt upright and her face flushed bright with spitting passion. 'Going to Mass is not going to help change you if you're a stinker!

'I've a terrible thing against hare coursing and I cannot reconcile the priests going to that and then saying Mass. I *could not go* to a church and listen to one of them speaking love and compassion. And the fact that the church has not spoken out against it *appals* me. Also the fact that they don't get more involved in cruelty to children. *Those* are the things they should be involved in. *Life*. And there are so many immoral things happening with moneylenders and people suffering – and they have nothing else to do but bloody sex because they have nowhere to *live* – the church should address themselves to *that*. Ordinary decent people looking for divorce. How *dare* they tell the women of Ireland what to do. It's not just the church, of course –'

As the storm raged, with names of organisations and individuals being battered by its fury, it was not difficult to see why good comics must first be straight dramatic actors who can call on deep passions but whose extra gift is for comic timing.

She apparently took anthropomorphism to extreme lengths, insisting that when a performing animal was hired for a Pantomime the producer, Fred O'Donovan, should take it on himself to be personally responsible for its welfare. 'Don't talk to me,' he says. 'If she could find an animal, from a donkey down – and cats. Don't talk to me about her and cats.' The theatre was home to lots of mice at one point so a cat was brought in. 'That cat didn't get a chance. She fed him the best of everything.

'She was absolutely, totally in love with animals; she used to drive me mad when I hired monkeys and elephants and all sorts; for instance once, when we had a monkey, she demanded that I give the monkey a dressing room, the same as any of the artists. So of course I had to.

'Next day I came in and found that the monkey had

dismantled every single one of the battery of lights around the mirrors. It cost me about two hundred pounds to get them fixed. And now this monkey unfortunately took a shine to me so she demanded that I had to look after it.

'Well, it got sick on the Saturday at the end of the first week. She was real worried about it: "There's only one thing to do. You take that monkey to the hospital, Fred!"'

So after the show, with monkey draped around his neck in loving but sick embrace, off Fred trudged to Mercer's Hospital at the end of South King Street. 'It was late. Only the blue lights on, every Saturday-night drunk in the place falling around, double-taking: "J – that's the hairiest looking child I ever saw!"'

Fred O'Donovan with monkey. Courtesy of Fred O'Donovan

'The Sister in charge fixed the monkey up, didn't cost her a thought, was used to me coming in with all sorts.

'Until I brought in a seal one time. I had to put a little reins on it. "What's wrong with the seal?" she asks me.

'"It's sick. It's not well. It's shitting all over the stage."

'"Ah, you should have given it a brandy and port."'

Once there was an elephant, housed in the orchestra pit. Mo Po sent someone out every day for a dozen fairy cakes and, before each show, fed them to the animal personally, one fairy cake at a time.

Like many other contributors to this book, the theatre producer Phyllis Ryan deplores the thoughtless, if well-meant, bandying of encomia when a prominent person dies: he/she was unique; the end of an era; we'll never see his/her like again …

She cast Maureen Potter alongside Siobhán McKenna in a celebrated production of *Arsenic and Old Lace* at the Gaiety and regards her personal experience of this run as the happiest and most rewarding of her professional life. In her piece, she sums up Maureen Potter's loss as follows:

'No, there will not be another like her. It *is* the end of an era and the world – a poor enough place as it stands – will feel emptier and we will be left to wonder if we "appreciated" enough all that she was and did for us and if we loved her enough and if we were truly thankful.'

Maureen Potter's assessment of the way she tried to live her life was aired in that interview of twenty years ago. She tried to live up to a maxim she discovered in a book, *Is There Life after Birth?* by Alexander King. The character is with his grandfather, who is dying, and is wondering if there is to be anything for him in the grandfather's will. 'I have nothing to leave you, son,' says the old man, 'except to say, "be delighted".'

She tried to be delighted, and was.

PART II

How Did she Do It?

Mamie Browne has a theory about Maureen Potter's unique, stentorian voice: 'When she was eight or nine, she ran into a wall and broke her nose and I always think that's where she got the funny voice, talking through her nose. She did sing, but I never thought she was a great singer ...'

The voice was only part of it: there were her expressive, plasticine-like features, her willingness to use every inch of her little body as if it were made of marla, *her timing – and that indefinable, very rare genetic quality of inherent comic talent.*

PAULINE MCLYNN

I had the great good fortune twice to work with Maureen at the Gate Theatre. The plays were *The School for Scandal* and *Tartuffe* and it was incredible to me, not only that I was appearing with one of the legends of Irish showbiz but also to find that she was the kindest, most generous woman in the town.

Ah now, don't get me wrong: you never stood on Maureen's laughs, upstaged her or acted the maggot while she was in full flight; but she returned the compliment, although she didn't need to – whenever Maureen came on stage you might as well go off and re-do your make-up for all the attention you got. The air became *electric* when she appeared. You knew she was there without even looking. Even strangers would poke one another and whisper because they too knew they were in the presence of a phenomenon. She was a giant (no mean feat for the tiniest of performers). And if you closed your eyes and just listened to her you'd swear she was ten-foot tall – which she was, in many ways.

The huge void in Irish entertainment left by Maureen's death underlines her importance and the enormous role she played in its development. She was probably the last of the great all-rounders. (And, yes, she could do it all.) She was probably also the last of the Great Stars.

I suppose it comes down to an individual and a particular

place in time: Maureen was trained up in variety, conquered comedy and moved on to lay waste to straight theatre, taking in radio, television and film on the way – all starting at a time when it was neither profitable nor fashionable to be a woman in those various worlds.

As a child of the sixties, I remember her, not for Panto (I grew up in Galway and we had no tradition of it and very little opportunity to travel for it while she was Queen), but for the incomparable 'Christy' sequences. The other women I saw being funny at the time were Lucille Ball and Carol Burnett, so I thought of Maureen in the same light and rightly so. She was pivotal to the rise of Irish women in comedy, though she may never have seen it quite that way.

There were two reasons for this, I think. The first was her modesty and the second was that I think she shattered the glass ceiling of 'the boys' club' without even noticing it was there. The consequence was that it was handily removed for all who came after her.

There was, of course, a Dark Side, as I liked to tell her from time to time. It was her involvement with the Third Reich. Before the war Maureen toured Europe and memorably performed one night before Hitler, Goebbels and Goering. Now, I'm not saying anything more than they loved the show and Hitler was very buoyed up after the event. Shortly afterwards, and still in great form altogether, he started World War II. 'Nuff said, draw your own conclusions ...

That being understood, let no one kid you about her achievements. They were huge and, as I've pointed out, *global*, accomplished solely by sheer dint of talent. For instance, a lot of people will posit the notion that comedy is all about timing – it's not: it's about being funny. Maureen was. She had funny bones. You cannot be taught that. Along with Jack, her husband, they poked merciless fun at pretension and politics and more. Nothing was beyond them or taboo; the only rule by which they played was that a gag be funny. In fact, at her funeral Jack wickedly and drolly remarked that he'd never seen so many *old* people – as a result there wasn't a dry leg in the house!

In addition to her comedic flair, Maureen also had the depth of intelligence and character to tackle O'Casey more successfully than anyone had in decades. Similarly, she shone in plays by Molière, Hugh Leonard, Sheridan – the list is too long to go into here. And to everything she touched she brought a magic that also could never be taught. There is no doubt but that she had 'It' – sometimes called star quality, a term too often abused.

'It' is something extra special, a bonus element to a personality, to do with self-belief and confidence but something more as well. 'It' is recognisable at the level of the subconscious, virtually indefinable, refusing to be dissected or explained. Its charisma is elusive but inescapable: think Bill Clinton,[*] Katherine Hepburn, our own Donal McCann. When It people enter a room or come on to a stage, they carry with them an extra dimension; they displace air; you don't know why, you just know that you are in the presence of excellence to a level encountered only rarely.

The quality transcends red carpets but beckons like a siren; it also keeps something back: Maureen Potter was everyone's friend, on stage and off, but outside her family, who really knew her?

Dammit, if we could bottle it we'd all be dangerous.

Where Maureen was concerned, all the rest of us could do was look and admire, and thank our lucky stars to have been up close to her a few times so we could bathe in reflected glory.

And now she's gone. We'll miss her for so many reasons – the laughs, the naughtiness, the sheer energy and joy of the woman. She was The Best and we'll not see her like again. We were delighted. Thank you, Mo.

---

[*] There is no real evidence that Maureen Potter had anything to do with the rise and fall of this man, unlike those she encountered in Germany (see above).

My abiding image of Maureen Potter is of her in an Irish dancing costume, with a scrunched-up expression of deep, concentrated pain and with a chestful of gongs, all bouncing in unison with her curly mop as she tripped through the jigs and the reels, arms and torso held excruciatingly rigid, feet flying and knees akimbo. It took decades to restore any credibility to Irish dancing after Maureen had finished with it, and not even *Riverdance* has completely expunged the Potterisation of the Baby Reel.

Maureen Irish dancing. Courtesy of Abhann

When I was a child, my mother would always call me to watch when Maureen Potter appeared on the television. Looking back on it, that says a lot about the kind of comedy she made. She was at one and the same time deeply subversive – remember the Carmelite habit? How did she get away with that in the devout sixties? And, come to think of it, *why* did we find it so funny – and completely acceptable? She held up a mirror to the Irish psyche, and we laughed at what we saw. It wasn't even a distorting mirror – it simply reflected the truth about ourselves – but there must have been something about the way she held that mirror, because it was deeply funny.

Any comic obviously has to be humorous, but Maureen Potter went one better than that. She was also good-humoured, which is quite a different thing, and a finer thing. She never just laughed at us: she made us laugh at ourselves, and she laughed along with us.

Ar dheis Dé ... I would say, only she would find some way of poking fun at that well-worn solemnity as well, but I mean it anyway.

GARRETT KEOGH

"'What is laughter?'
(pause)
"'The one thing that separates man from animals,'
said Dr Johnson
(pause)
"'who'd never heard of hyenas.'"

> *Hancock's Last Half-Hour* by Heathcote
> Williams.(The pauses are mine.)

Comedy, tragedy, two ends of the one stick. Tragedy says we're human and hopeless; comedy says it's hopeless trying to be anything else.

But comedy is harder to do than tragedy. For an actor it's easier to be sad than happy; it's harder to make them laugh than cry. The energy is different, the quality of time is different. And it's all about time. Very often a patron will ask: 'How do you remember all the words?'

The stock reply: 'The words are easy to learn, the pauses between them are hard.'

That's what you do in rehearsal, you try to find the pause.

You mess about with time, you try the line this way and that. Do you leave a beat here – or there? What feels like it fits? It's instinct and skill, it's individual and collective. You might not always know what's right, but you'll nearly always know when it's wrong. And when it is, you scrub that attempt and you start all over again.

Then you take all these moments, these pauses you've built, string them together, breathe life into them and invite an audience to share in the time you've made. The suspension of disbelief? The illusion of harnessing time.

In tragedy the pause can be more passive – some of the saddest pauses are unintentional – but in comedy it has to be active. A deadpan is the stubborn look that grits its teeth and says: I will not give you the satisfaction of showing you just how annoying, boring, insignificant and irritatingly ignorant I find you. It's a state of denial that says I am totally unaffected, while at the same time allowing an audience a glimpse of the volcano that's rumbling inside. And a slow-burn is just that, it's a fire that's slowly rippling under the surface just waiting to explode.

In tragedy there's fall, there's loss; we recognise the inexorable hand of Fate. In comedy, the same, except it's a pratfall, it's a banana skin waiting to trip you up. The more the audience knows it's going to happen, and the more the actor tries in vain to prevent it, the funnier it is. If you try to best gravity, if your arm windmills and your feet fly while you try to keep your balance, if your body spins helplessly like you're skating on ice, it's funny. If your legs scissor in the air as you fall on your bum, then it's funnier still. And it's hilarious if you're amused or surprised, if you let on it didn't happen, if you try to smile through the pain. Nobody expects the tragic hero to laugh, but if you want to be funny you've got to show teeth and eyes.

There's an old saying that you do comedy in white light, because they have to see your eyes. They have to be sure. Tragedy and comedy are so close you have to let the audience know. You have to say: *it's OK to laugh*. (Why are the simple things always so hard?) You have to be clear, in action, tone and voice. There's no room for waffle or fluff. Every last detail is intended, every moment precise. All night, every night you have to be fresh like it's never happened before. If you want to make people laugh you have to be sharp, you have to be on your toes. And you have to make that concentration and effort look like it's not work at all. You have to enjoy it.

It's a paradox: you must be relaxed, put the audience at ease, make them feel they've all the time in the world, while you are so energised, so animated, so alert, so desperate, that every moment might be your last.

This is a skill that can't be taught. Schools can teach methods, they can develop techniques, but they can't manufacture talent or instinct; and every method, every technique is merely a tool, a clue; it's the beginning of a map that might help you find the way on your own. You learn from doing it. You learn on your feet. You learn by going red in the face when you're wrong. And you learn by doing it with others who have done it before.

Twice I soldiered with Mo Po. First in *Arsenic and Old Lace* with her and Siobhán McKenna at the Gaiety. And then on tour with *Juno and the Paycock*: the Edinburgh Festival, Jerusalem and Broadway in a heat wave.

One evening after the *Arsenic* rehearsal, I asked Liam Sweeney to go for a drink. (Liam – there was more meat on a butcher's apron – had been Uncle Peter in *The Plough and the Stars* at the Abbey, and I was the Covey who thwarted him. He loved it so much he carried it with him onto the street. 'Cuckoo! Cuckoo!' he'd shout whenever he saw me.) But this evening he declined: he had a lift going home. The next morning he didn't come in. He was found drowned at the edge of the canal. Everyone was stunned. But we went on, an assorted company of romantics, rogues and vagabonds; two old dears burying bodies in the cellar and me, their unlikely, unhinged brother, all trying to make people laugh.

Ray McAnally used to say that acting was about making a change in the eyes; the eyes of the other actor. Philip

O'Flynn did it to me when I was younger, scared me witless with a pause. In *Arsenic*, Maureen and I stood downstage centre in her Gaiety Theatre. She said her line and set my line up like a golf ball sitting on a tee waiting to be whacked. Skill, poise, grace and generosity. Her delivery demanded attention, demanded my thought. She made it, made the pause, made the time. All I had to do was attend. And when I spoke, the house collapsed in laughter.

In *Juno*, she danced life into Maisie Madigan. She displaced air (as Ray McAnally said in another context, but that's another story). 'Don't drown it Johnny!' she shrieked in *alto soprano* panic when Donal McCann's Captain Boyle watered her whiskey. But you could feel the stillness in the air in the silence she made at the death.

We were in the Mound in Edinburgh one day. It was packed with performers and crowds milling round the street-theatre shows. Fire-eaters, jugglers, bands, acrobats, skirling bagpipes played by punk rockers in kilts wearing nose rings and multi-coloured Mohicans. She beamed with delight when she found a makeshift booth that advertised individual poetry readings. A small version of a Punch and Judy stand, candy-striped canvas, a blackboard at the side listed its wares: Shakespeare, Blake, Donne, Keats and so on. In the mayhem that was the Mound she never gave it a second thought. 'You'd have to support your own,' she said. She paid the money, pulled up the stool, leaned in and asked for *The Lake Isle of Inisfree*. 'The only Irish one he had,' she said. 'I told him he should get some more.'

Her husband came with her on that tour. In hotel lobbies, restaurants, milk bars and coffee shops, in residents' lounges, airports, buses and diners, she sat, perched, beside Jack, twinkle toes dangling on the ends of her little legs. Those legs had seen some service and they knew it. (Flatley might hold the world record for taps per second, but Potter's dancing feet win the laughing stakes hands down.) Philip O'Flynn used to say it was a medical fact that an actor's first-night nerves were equivalent to the trauma of minor surgery. In

Panto and *Gaels*, in play, sketch and revue, how many operations did Mo undergo in the cause? 'Nobody knows what I'm going through with the pains in these legs of mine,' Captain Boyle says again and again. But Potter was too generous for that. She had more concern. She had more sense. She shared food and drink, swapped jokes and stories, gossiped, groused – all the things you do on tour – but she kept her pains to herself. And when the off-stage dramas turned to crises she never lost the cool, never judged. She saved her breath and continued giving, smiling, encouraging.

Those dramas included Breaking and Entering, Operation Tel Aviv, The Misnomer of the Hotel Shalom, The Battle of Broadway, The Boys in Dressing room 8 and The Manhattan Cat and the Moon. She laughed when I told her the story of The Incident at Heathrow. *En route* to Jerusalem there were British bobbies with machine guns and dogs patrolling the El Al waiting lounge. We were brought into a big room and, one on one, were asked to account for our hand luggage. Is this yours? Did you pack it yourself? Did anybody ask you to carry anything for them? The young man beside me asked Geraldine Plunkett if she knew why he was asking these questions. Yes, she said, for safety, for security. Specifically, he replied, because a fellow-countrywoman of yours was recently found bringing a bomb onto one of our planes. 'Oh yes,' said Geraldine, 'she lives around the corner from me in Sallynoggin!'

'Security begins at home,' said Mo.

The Burial at Thebes was on at the Abbey when she died. At the curtain I spoke of her extraordinary talent; how she was great company. She was our colleague, I said, and had worked on this stage. I asked the audience to join with us in the custom of applauding her final exit.

The play she did there was Hugh Leonard's *Moving*. One day, when they were rehearsing, she and Johnny Murphy went to lunch. They went to The Flowing Tide. They had a 'sandwich'. It was a special day: Lord Snowdon was coming in to take snaps.

She was nervous coming back up in the lift. They were five minutes late; everyone was waiting. The tripod was set. The Abbey rehearsal room looked very serious and formal. Suddenly our bright spark dived in. All four-foot-something of her looked up at the British Royal stood tall on the rostrum: 'I'm sorry we're late, my Lord. But I worked for a long time with a great man, James A. O'Dea. And one day he was late coming back to rehearsal. What kept him? He had been to the bookies ... And when he was leaving this stranger grabbed him by the arm.' She took a pause, pouted her lips, fluttered her innocent eyes, struck a Feis Ceoil pose and said in a crystal clear, politely posh, gloriously irreverent voice:

> Did it ever occur to you?
> That as you get old your balls go cold,
> The top of your cock it turns blue,
> It bends in the middle like a Japanese fiddle;
> Did it ever occur to you?

There is a bench with a plaque in her honour in the Merrion cricket ground on Anglesea Road. (She loved the game and was patron of the Theatrical Cavaliers, the actors' cricket club.) On summer evenings by the Dodder bank, old ghosts can sit and sip sandwiches to the pit-pat of willow on leather as the sun goes down.

And when a thespian in whites vainly chases a ball panting to the boundary, he might recognise the twinkle toes dangling, that down-the-nose comic disdain, the slow-turning gaze (creating the pause) directing his eyes towards the engraving: *Save your breath to cool your porridge!*

PART III

Going to the Panto

Going to the Pantomime en famille *was a constant theme for contributors and in the present era of DVDs, texting, picture phones and Sunday outings to shopping malls the image of family life that emerges is not only nostalgic, but telling. Listening to Potter on the radio by the fireside or visiting her as an annual event was part of the family calendar. The name of the individual Panto or show did not matter and to go 'to Maureen Potter' (and, before her takeover as solo headliner, 'Jimmy O'Dea-and-Maureen Potter'), parish coach outings were organised and CIÉ even offered special train fares from mainline stations around the country. Some of these contributions naturally cover the same territory – Christy on his balloon flight features quite a bit – yet each contributor adds very personal and distinctive detail: a specific ritual made of the outing or the use of a specific mode of transport – for instance, the sculptor John Behan remembers careering around St Stephen's Green in a sand lorry. There were 'treat' trips to posh hotels for meals before the show, while huge delight was taken in the unusual behaviour of a mother or father hitherto seen, perhaps, as remote or harassed. There is intense sensory recall on hearing even a mention of the comedienne's name: the author Patricia Scanlan could immediately smell mushy peas; for actor and writer Donal O'Kelly, his skin experienced again the torturous, scratchy feel of a new duffle-coat made from corduroy as hard as iron.*

The chairman of the Abbey Theatre, Eithne Healy, initially at a loss to decide how to honour the talent and personality of an artist she had venerated all her life, eventually decided simply to write directly to the dead star, telling what was in her heart. In doing so, she not only paid her tribute, but layered another patina on the image of a very particular period in Irish family life.

My dear Maureen,

I owe you a great debt of thanks because, as was the case with most Dubliners, you were my introduction to theatre, which has played such a rich part in my life.

My late father, George, who was in the rag trade, worked in South King Street (in the premises that is now called STOCK) and because he supplied shirts to the musicians in the Gaiety Theatre Orchestra, he got invitations to the shows there and never missed a performance. My mother, May, was not keen on theatre (she found Jimmy O'Dea a bit off colour) so I accompanied George and thus began my love affair with the stage.

I have wonderful memories of those outings. They became quite ritualistic. The Morris Minor was driven into the warehouse on South King Street, then we went to Peter's Pub – a glass of Club Orange for me, a pint of Guinness for George – but we had to arrive in the theatre in time to hear the orchestra tuning up; in his spare time, George played a mean clarinet.

The Panto and *Gaels of Laughter* were firm favourites. The theatre always seemed to be packed for those performances, and the wave of affection that greeted your arrival on stage was pure magic. The political monologues and the 'Christy' sketches between the big musical numbers kept everyone happy, and it came as no surprise to me to hear you say on radio, years later, that your mantra for everyone was 'Be delighted'. How simple. How successful!

Our paths crossed on a more personal level in the mid-eighties when, during my tenure on the board of the Dublin Theatre Festival, you played Martha in the Festival's production of *Arsenic and Old Lace* to Siobhan McKenna's Abby. You two *grandes dames* of the theatre packed the Gaiety for a month, every night a triumph. I was often around the green room on those evenings and witnessed you mothering the large cast: had they eaten? How were they getting home? Were they getting enough sleep? You were caring about everyone except yourself, although the arthritis was already bothering you.

I was fortunate to go on tour with the Gate Theatre production of *Juno and the Paycock*, with John Kavanagh, Geraldine Plunkett, the late Donal McCann and yourself as Maisie Madigan. The *Irish Times* critic David Nowlan described this as the definitive *Juno* and gave it his special accolade of 'go see'.

You had, of course, acted before in straight plays, for

instance in the Edwards/MacLíammóir productions, but for a new generation of theatre-goers this was the first time to see you in a straight role. It was a huge hit, not least in New York.

And Jerusalem. At that time, Jerusalem was not a great tourist destination – the hotels and the food were not good – but what an amazing time we all had; people are what matter, and we had such a wonderful group of people along on that tour. We did all the sights, and I remember you being photographed on a (not-too-docile) camel! What laughs we had!

I was there, cheering you on when there were many formal tributes paid to you over the years – The National Entertainment Award, the wonderful tribute evening at the Gaiety (where else?) when that stunning portrait of you by James Hanley was hung in the foyer. There was that Honorary Doctorate of Letters from Trinity College, and I particularly remember the day you received the Freedom of the City in the Mansion House, when traffic came to a standstill around St Stephen's Green because Dawson Street was mobbed by your fans. To be honoured in your own city and have your own fans thronging – it does not get much better than that, Maureen!

One word describes all of these occasions – love. You loved what you did. And everyone loved you.

The last time we met was at the special tribute *Late Late Show* with Pat Kenny to celebrate the Abbey Theatre Centenary, where, in your usual sparkling form, you sang a song in your inimitable style and paid generous tributes to your colleagues at the Abbey, although you had played in only one production there, *Moving* by Hugh Leonard. That did not matter at all because you had crossed all theatrical boundaries.

You were a star, Maureen, and your legacy will remain in our hearts forever. We miss your presence; Jack must miss you most of all.

My husband, Liam, with whom you had so many happy chats, joins me in thanking you both for your friendship.

Affectionately,

Eithne.

Maureen with Vernon Hayden. Photo: Michael O'Reilly

DONAL O'KELLY

It starts with a pattern. In the lull. That mixed-up week between Stephen's Day and New Year's Eve.

In the dusky late afternoon, a big fold-out sheet of thin, greyish tissue-paper comes out of a cardboard envelope and soon it covers the breakfast-room lino. Dotted lines have little scissors signs on them. A new thing called a pinking-shears, a scissors with teeth, attacks the dotted lines. They curve away from it. On the front of the cardboard envelope there's a picture. Of a duffle-coat, arms out, hood up, no one in it.

Two days later, a real duffle-coat stands on its own in the middle of the breakfast-room floor. Its material is so thick it doesn't need anyone to stand inside it. It does it by itself. I put it on. It's like armour. I'd have to be hoisted onto my bike wearing it.

The toggles are the last thing to be put on. My mother has a thing, halfway between chalk and soap, that makes a mark when she rubs it on the material to tell her where to sew the toggles. But the toggles are made out of tusk or something, like mini rhino horns. 'Very tough,' she says. And they're tied onto the duffle-coat with leather. So she has to use a huge needle Gramma gave her to go through the folded-over leather and her eyebrows join and she says 'tshuh, tshuh' because it hurts her fingers.

When the main toggles are done, she says that'll have to do for now, because she hasn't time to put on the second row of toggles, which are just for balance and decoration. She rushes to sew two little buttons onto the bit that goes across my mouth. But I'm getting worried now. It's nearly seven o'clock. The Panto starts at eight. It's Maureen Potter night again. And my duffle-coat is lovely, really. But it'll do now. It doesn't need anything else done to it. Still she sews two little buttons on the bit that goes across my mouth to keep the hood tight around my ears. Then we all run out the door, with Edward from across the road with us as well.

New duffle-coat and Maureen Potter go together every year.

Inside the glass doors of the Gaiety it's bright and packed

and hot and the taste of the stiff hood-buttoner is starting to make me feel a bit sick now because I can't open it to get the hood off. The buttons are too tight. Panic for a minute, then relief as Edward gets it off for me. The time has come. We smile at the big man in the major's uniform who stands taking the tickets at the stairs to the Grand Circle. Back again, he says, or something, big beam. Mam smiles and says 'Oh yes' and he winks at me and Edward. There's a reason for this and we know what it is. We smile back at him. And we go on up. It's a great ruse. Because me and Edward only take up one seat. We always get the same special seats. Front row, top tier. There's the aisle, then four seats in a row, then a small gap where there's nothing and then a little wall you can look over, curving around where you come in. Edward and me take turns, one of us sitting in the seat, the other wedged in the space between the seat and the little wall. It's great. We both prefer being wedged half-way on our hunkers. My duffle-coat lies along the little wall ...

Even the safety curtain is fantastic. It has ads painted on it for Kennedy's Bread and Smiths' Crisps and some other things. And you can see the band people talking to each other. They come out of a secret tunnel. Then the safety curtain goes up.

And we roar laughing. At Maureen Potter. I think it's *Robin Hood* or maybe *Aladdin* or something else, they're all mixed up on me now. But she skips in and everyone laughs and claps. We love it. We love her. She bounces around the place. As if she has little jets of air coming out the soles of her feet propelling her upwards. She can do scissors-steps in mid-air like the pinking-shears. She says 'boys and girls' like no-one else says it. Her mouth goes small then wide, small then wide. We're in her gang.

She asks us to keep an eye out. For the bad fella. And then, of course, when it's dangerous and she thinks he's gone away, he comes out of a secret door right behind her. And she's whistling away and talking to us.

For God's sake! *He's right behind you.*

And she says 'What?' as if she's deaf. And then I tell her because everyone else is telling her as well and she mustn't be able to hear because it's just a big noise. It's ridiculous, but it's scary too, even though I know it's the Pantomime. He's going to get her unless she stops fooling around. And she's all blow-cheeked oh-one-side-and-oh-the-other-side. So I try to say it loud and clear so there can be no mistake. But just as I start to say it, everyone else stops. I don't know why. And I've started so I finish. 'He's behind you!' And suddenly my voice echoes all over the Gaiety. On its own. Just me. Roaring like a lunatic.

Why did everyone stop? Did I miss something? Some people are looking up at me from the lower tier. And they're all laughing. Then Maureen Potter looks up at me. Her eyes go huge, she makes a big 'O' with her mouth and she asks me if I said he was behind her? But I'm saying nothing now. Head down. I must have missed a vital bit.

But then, just as he's about to grab her, she runs out of his grasp. And the chase is on. Someone helps her in another door. And then she comes up a trapdoor. And then she's flying over their heads. And now she has a different 'O' on her mouth. It's a brave 'O', not an afraid 'O'. Still someone else to save so they can marry or something, but she's going to win now. I saved Maureen Potter from the bad fella, I think. Unless there's something I missed.

Then there's a bit where she's sitting on a bench smoking a fag with Danny Cummins. They were charwomen gabbing. And there was stuff that my mother went 'Oh yes!' at and had to hold her cheekbones it was so funny – but yet it was true. About the politicians. Edward and me liked it just as much as if we knew what it was all about. Did the bad fella come up behind them again or am I getting mixed up?

And then a lady in a kind of a gym-slip with flowing golden hair like Niamh Cinn Óir did head-over-heels backwards on a horsey thing and stood upside-down on her hands and all, but even more things, and we all clapped when she did little bits of it and then lifted up her arms, and it was only when it was nearly over that we all looked at each other and said, 'My God that's *her*, that's Maureen Potter!' And my mother was amazed that she could do all that at her age. A-*mazed*.

And then she had this big bit where her son, Christy, got caught on a balloon and went sailing off up into the air and she was running after him trying to get him down; away off up over Dublin he went, and something about 'Not the Rotunda, Christy, anywhere else but not the Rotunda.' I still don't get the joke but the Gaiety must have nearly fallen down everybody laughed so loud, and Edward and me were crying we thought it was so funny with her big eyes and her big 'O' on her mouth and what was going to happen to poor Christy?

And at the end we're getting tired, thinking about getting the chips on the way home same as every year and putting the duffle-coat on again: will I do it inside or wait until I get outside where there's more room to move around? Trying to catch the sticky-out sleeves –

And they all come out for the big ending, and then another big ending in their wedding costumes, and then Maureen Potter, the smallest of them all, steps forward and says, same as every year, about if you liked it, tell your friends, and if you didn't – save – your breath – to cool – your porridge! And a shut mouth – catches no flies!

Oh she's fantastic, we all say. That was the best yet. Maureen Potter is the best there is. My God! And we tell the Christy bit to each other over and over again – where he went to in the balloon and the stupid things he tried to do, the thick; we talk about it all the way home. When the car windows fog up from the chips and the lovely smell of the hot paper, it's as if Maureen Potter is still with us right there in the car and we'd love to bring her in and put the rest of the chips out on plates to eat them properly and give her a cup of tea. The only problem is she'd have to be like Santy and be in every house in Dublin at the same time, and my duffle-coat, which I have to wriggle off over my head because I'm too tired to open the toggles, bows to the Queen of Dublin Pantomime.

Next year, the duffle-coat will be old and torn and a new duffle-coat stiff in its place, but Maureen Potter will be out there when the safety curtain goes up again with her big eyes and her way of saying 'boys and girls' and her mouth in a huge big 'O' that would make us laugh all our life long.

Maureen (Sr Philomena), Jim Bartley and Dorothy Paul.
Photo: Michael O'Reilly

MARITA CONLON-McKENNA

Long before there was Harry Potter, there was another 'Potter' wizard who could work magic and enchant millions of children all over Ireland. That wizard was Maureen Potter, who had the power to entertain and – with her own magic – enthral every child lucky enough to get a magic ticket to sit in the audience at one of her shows.

Every Christmas we joined that lucky group! My sister Gerardine and I were buffled into our heavy winter coats, patent shoes and best party dresses by my mother and my aunt and brought to Dublin's Gaiety Theatre see the Panto. *Puss in Boots, Aladdin, Dick Whittington, Cinderella,* all the storybook classics, but it made no difference to us what the story was as there was no doubt in any of our minds as to who the true hero was – it was Maureen Potter, the elfin woman with the big eyes who danced around the stage and made us laugh.

Walking across the plush carpet of the Gaiety Theatre we knew immediately that we had stepped into a different world. Waiting for the curtain to rise, a huge cheer and roar of approval filled the place when Maureen first appeared on stage. Because of her height, she always seemed one of us and like the Pied Piper. We were prepared to follow wherever she would lead us. She could sing and dance and be funny all at the same time! She held us in the palm of her hand as she rattled off stories that made us rock with laughter. No one dared to go to the toilet once Maureen was on stage for fear of missing something funny and wonderful; better to cross our legs and wait for the dancing girls or the hero's song solo.

My sister and I cringed when she talked about our school and 'The Little Sisters of the Rich up in Mount Anville'; and we didn't know whether to blush or sit up proudly when sometimes our dad's business got a mention.

Every show, a host of names and schools and identifiable people were tumbled out, all as a result of her incredible antenna, so she knew who was in her audience. *Did she ask the box-office lady who was buying tickets?*

Summers were even better, for in *Gaels of Laughter* the whole show revolved around Maureen!

Once the good weather came, we moved down to our house in Greystones, Co. Wicklow, and every year my sister and I joined in many of the family outings of our next-door neighbours the Ryans.

Dr Ryan, a country G.P., was, as my father called him, 'a gentleman'. He was quiet and thoughtful, sitting smoking his cheroots looking out at the sea over his daily *Irish Times*. A kind man with a generous heart, he joined his family for the month of August and planned a round of activities for his brood – and often the two little girls next door.

There were enormous picnics on the Sugar Loaf, fishing trips in his boat, day trips on the Mail Boat to Holyhead (coming home laden with Anglesey rock and bags of Opal Fruits) but to my mind the very best excursion and treat of the summer, kept till last, was the annual visit to *Gaels of Laughter*, the Gaiety's summer show.

We all got dressed up for the occasion, the girls in summer dresses, the boys – hair clipped and combed or crew cut – in neat trousers and shirts, as we squashed into the family Rover. Dr Ryan and his wife always insisted on dinner first in the Russell Hotel overlooking Stephen's Green, reminding us we were young ladies and gentlemen as we entered the fashionable restaurant. The doorman greeted us like we were long lost friends, then Doctor Ryan told us to order what we liked from the vast menu.

My sister and I felt like princesses, the Ryan boys transformed to young princes, as we sat down at the huge table, all the grown ups around us wondering who was mad enough to bring such a huge crowd of kids to a good restaurant. Scampi, prawns, steak, roast lamb, we tried them all, followed by pineapple or apple fritters and ice-cream – a speciality of the house!

Then, like a load of ducklings, we were marched around The Green and up to South King Street to the Gaiety Theatre, up the stairs and into the large balcony overlooking the stage. My sister and I almost sick with excitement as down below us the orchestra warmed up.

Tommy, the youngest Ryan boy, was devoted to Maureen and every year, like a young beau, would purchase a bunch of flowers and a big box of chocolates to present to her either before the show, during the interval or after final curtain. The rest of us were sick with jealousy when he disappeared off to meet Maureen and talk to her.

On his return we hung on his every word as, eyes shining, he gave us a blow-by-blow account of her reaction and what she said to him. (He was looking so-o handsome in his shirt – or jacket or tie – in fact, he was the perfect and wonderful young gentleman. Looking back it was all designed to make him feel ten feet tall.)

During the show Maureen would always give a great mention to her young friend Tommy. She would thank him and throw a few sweets up in our direction. All of us there in the balcony basked in the glow of her attention. She had the most incredible memory and, at the end of every show, listed everyone who was lucky enough to have a birthday – so that my sister and I secretly cursed our November and February birth dates.

She sang songs about everything and to our amazement would put in things that were only just in the news, making our parents hysterical.

At the time we were growing up, all the funny people in comedy on the stage and TV and films were men who were fast and clever and told funny stories. I knew that my aunt, and Mrs Glynn next door, and some of my friends' mothers were funny, but for some reason female comedians were in short supply. Women who were funny were scarce and usually were laughed at for being fat or their bust size or their stupidity! Maureen was different. She made us laugh with her words and quick wit and sense of Dublin humour.

Sometimes she dressed up as a nun or a hippy, a schoolgirl, a cleaning lady or a policewoman doing a routine, often with Danny Cummins; but other times she stood on that big stage all alone with no wig or fancy make-up, in a black or navy velvet trouser suit and told us stories which made us laugh so hard that the tears rolled down our faces.

My favourite character of hers was Christy's mammy.

Christy was a Dublin boy who got into more trouble than we ever did! He had his poor mammy's heart scalded with his antics and she always seemed to be running around on her little legs chasing after him. The day Christy got some free 'balloo-oons' was a classic.

'Hang on to them balloo-oons, son!' warned his mammy, so Christy hung on tight, really tight, as the wind lifted him up off his feet and he floated off up O'Connell Street. Not to be defeated the mammy chases after him, praying that the Irish Air Force or Aer Lingus will help catch him: 'Christy,' she yelled, 'be careful of them pigeons!' – but too late, the pigeons had done their worst …

At the end of the show, there was always a big finale when all the cast came on one after another to take a bow. We reserved our loudest cheers for our heroine, Maureen, nearly bringing the roof of the old theatre down with our applause.

She would stand there and clap at us for being a good audience and then there would be a hush as we listened to her final words urging us, like the master showman she was, if we liked the show to go and tell our friends and neighbours and if we didn't to 'Save your breath to cool your porridge!'

As the final curtain came down and the stage emptied we blinked, unbelieving, the magic over, the wizard gone, disappeared until the next time.

To this day I cannot see a stray balloon adrift in the sky without thinking of Christy and his mammy and the amazing warm-hearted, generous-spirited woman who conjured up such stories and entertainment for generations of Irish children to enjoy.

JOHN CREEDON

My Dad loved Maureen Potter. Had they ever met, I'm sure Maureen would have loved him too. They shared a love of the important things in life – children, dogs and a good ol' belly-laugh. He was a big man, and his tummy danced a jig every time he laughed, so it was *céilí* time every time Maureen was on.

I remember, growing up in Cork in the sixties, how he would cajole us to '*Hush!*' whenever she appeared on the old black and white Pilot television. Similarly, he would 'hiren the wireless' so the whole street could hear her any time she performed on radio.

He would also nod his approval at every gag. I used say to him that nodding at someone on the telly was madness, but nodding at someone on the *radio* was even worse. I don't think he got it!

I never asked him why he admired her so much, but I expect it was because she was a woman in a man's domain. As father to eight daughters, he fostered an independent attitude and always admired 'feisty women'. So, the sight of a workin' class Dub threatenin' to kill 'Christea' if he didn't 'come in fo' his dinnah' was a source of great joy to him.

I moved to Dublin in 1987 to work with RTÉ and 'No Dad, not yet' was my reply the first dozen times he enquired if I had got to meet Maureen Potter. Eventually I did get to meet Maureen Potter and he squeezed every detail of the encounter from me.

'Sure, I'll organise a private audience for you some day,' I promised. And I did try. However he had to go to a funeral in Cork on the night I had booked us into the show in Clontarf Castle. The opportunity passed and before long my Dad had passed on, and now Maureen has too.

However, I trust that by now they're swapping gags in that great green room in the sky.

I could never claim to have been a close personal friend of Maureen Potter, but we did work together on TV a few times and she also guested on my radio show. But somehow she was part and parcel of our kitchen in Cork and when, on the day she died, they replayed some of those old sketches on the news, I found myself nodding along in encouragement, just as my father had.

God rest them both.

SARAH WEBB

I am eternally grateful to Maureen Potter, because without her I would never have been taken to the Pantomime and I would have missed out on one of childhood's greatest pleasures.

I should explain: my father is a lover of the old school of comedy – Morecambe and Wise, Bruce Forsyth's *Generation Game*, *The Two Ronnies* – and he also loved Maureen Potter with a passion. He would wait patiently during the Panto-mime, children giggling hysterically, screaming and shouting all around him, for Maureen's special and finely tuned rant about Ireland and its politicians/bankers/roads – whatever took her fancy that particular year.

My sisters and I would lean back in our seats during the 'adults' bit', as we called it, and argue over who got the last mini-Dairy Milk bar from the box of chocolates, while Dad listened in rapt attention to Maureen, guffawing, snorting loudly and even slapping his leg in mirth, much to our collective amusement. I don't recall Mum being at any of the Pantomimes (sorry Mum, I know you must have been present for at least some of them), as it was Dad's special treat to 'his girls', along with visiting Santa in Switzers, driving up and down O'Connell Street to see the sparkly white Christmas lights on the trees and having a slap-up meal of sausages and chips in Bewley's; sometimes all done in one frenzied, glorious rush on the very same December day.

The Maureen Potter Pantomimes have left an indelible memory in my mind – one of laughter, delight, wonderment and astonishment. To this day I can still see the lights, the wonderfully over-the-top stage make-up and the dazzling, sparkling costumes, which impressed me no end. I still remember vividly the groups of all-singing and all-dancing children, the Billy Barry Kids I seem to recall, and am in complete awe of their precocious talent …

And the handsome leading men on whom I always developed a bit of a crush – which lasted at least two weeks: far longer than any of my pop star crushes.

But more than anything, I remember Maureen Potter, *uber* Panto Dame, who made my Dad laugh so much. To be honest, I don't think I've heard him laugh quite so heartily or so genuinely since.

SHEILA O'FLANAGAN

I'm of that generation of children who grew up with Maureen Potter. Both *Gaels of Laughter* and the Christmas

Pantomime were big events in our house and among the only times we went out as a family, dressed up to the nines for a big occasion. Getting ready took half the day and my parents used to tell us that as we were going to the theatre we had to be on our absolute best behaviour or we'd be thrown out. It was probably the only time they managed to get all three of their daughters to sit down together without picking a fight.

One year my Dad, as a special treat, got us a box in the Gaiety for *Gaels*. We felt totally privileged to be sitting high up in the theatre, with a great view of the stage, instead of having to crane our necks to see what was going on. That year was also the year that Maureen Potter called out my sister's name in her birthday list at the end of the show. She said Joan's name as though her greatest wish was that Joan O'Flanagan would have the happiest birthday of anyone in Ireland that day. We all got a great thrill out of it and Joan was, naturally, insufferable for days afterwards!

When I was younger, of course, it was all about the Pantomimes. And what I remember most about them was that (even when we weren't lucky enough to have the box) I could always hear and understand every single word that Maureen Potter spoke. She involved me totally in what was going on in front of me.

Later, when I was a little older, I remember 'getting' my first political joke at *Gaels of Laughter* and sharing the wit of it with both my parents, feeling very grown up. I realised then that Maureen's talent lay in appealing to everyone in the audience at many different levels of enjoyment.

I never saw her act in any serious roles, though I know she received great critical acclaim for these. To me, and I'm quite sure to countless other people like me, she will always be caught up with the biggest family day out of the year, when all of us laughed with her and went home happy, satisfied and feeling as though we'd got our money's worth.

And we never had to save our breath to cool our porridge.

Two things will always remind me of childhood Sunday lunches: the name Maureen Potter and the cooking smells of mushy marrowfat peas.

Radio was very important in our house. We didn't have a TV as, in their wisdom, our parents felt it stunted the imagination. They had watched as their six lively offspring turned into square eyes and couch potatoes and, much to our dismay, got rid of the offending article.

Two radio programmes were sacrosanct: the Michael P. O'Connor story at tea-time on Wednesday and *The Maureen Potter Show* at midday on Sunday.

I remember wet Sundays sitting in the kitchen on the little red seat beside the blazing fire, listening to the unique and irrepressible Maureen yell 'Christyyyyyyyyy!' while, over at the cooker, the roast beef and roast potatoes would sizzle in the oven and the mushy peas would bubble under the watchful gaze of my mother. (It was fatal to take your eyes off them or they would boil over with volcanic abandon, ruining the top of the cooker and stinking out the kitchen.)

'What do you mean you got no homework?' Maureen would yell at the hapless Christy. And we'd all guffaw in delight at our hero's trials and tribulations.

The Panto at Christmas was, of course, a big treat. I'd be sick with excitement as we queued up at the box-office for our tickets for the afternoon matinée. Sitting in the red velvet, faintly shabby seats made me feel so grown up. The mounting excitement as we waited for the lights to dim and the curtain to rise! Then the drum roll and the curtain slowly rising and there she was – a magic, vibrant, lively sprite leaping around the stage as the crowd roared its delight at seeing her.

How we loved yelling 'Oh no he didn't!' to her 'Oh yes he did!' How my parents would laugh at her incisive, witty, but never malicious barbs directed towards the politicians of the day.

I remember at one show gazing in awe as Patricia Cahill,

an ethereal Princess, sang 'Moonlight and Roses' in a duet with Maureen. There wasn't a sound in the packed theatre. (I sang that song for six months afterwards, trilling the highest notes *à la* Patricia Cahill until I nearly drove my poor mother mad.) Every year, exhilarated, the six of us would leave the Gaiety full of plans for a Panto of our own.

An added treat as we drove down the rarefied environs of Grafton Street were the Christmas lights and the window display in Switzers – the poshest shop in Dublin.

Maureen Potter and Christmas lights. What more could a child ask for? It was our day of enchantment.

I was one of a generation for whom the name Maureen Potter meant laughter, giddy excitement and most of all magic. Wasn't I lucky?

Maureen and Jimmy O'Dea as hunters.
Photo: The O'Dea Collection @ The Irish Theatre Archive

When I reflect on my childhood Christmases, there are some particular memories that I hold very precious to this day. Images of visits to Santa in Clery's on O'Connell Street (hustle, bustle, warmth, energy, the luscious red carpet covering the magnificent staircase guiding us to Mr Claus and his many treasures) come flooding vividly back.

For my brother, Seán, and myself, those visits to Clery's were something we looked forward to with great anticipation and excitement – but what I now look back on with special fondness are the suppers in the Savoy Theatre or Gresham Hotel, followed by a visit to Maureen Potter and Jimmy O'Dea in the Gaiety Theatre.

My father was a great fan of Maureen and Jimmy together; my mother loved Maureen herself to bits; but for my brother and me, these performances were an introduction to the theatre. I loved every part of the experience – the dressing up, the magnificence of the theatre, the buzz of the crowd – in fact the whole event was such a special treat, with Maureen's performance, no matter what role she played, as the culmination of a magical experience. She was everywhere, running around the stage, encouraging us all to participate; I clearly remember the exhilaration at being allowed – even encouraged – to scream and shout back at her.

To be honest, when I think of Maureen Potter now, I am reminded, not only of those magical nights, but also of the wonder of childhood, the love and energy of my mother and father, the warmth of our family unit, the certainty, the joy of sharing. I find myself being transported into pictures of the past, of Mommy and Daddy loving our reactions to the Panto and encouraging our dreams, of my father making sure that the wonder we got from Maureen's performances in the theatre was kept alive when we got home by encouraging us to play out scenes of our own in order to develop our imagination.

So Christmas for me holds all these wonderful memories, nostalgia for things past and a sense that things will never be the same again. We tried to create that same atmosphere with our children but I think the competition was too great; media was very much a part of my kids' world and, while Maureen Potter was a part of their lives too and they really enjoyed her shows, times had changed too much for that same magic to be recreated for them.

They have created their own recollections, ways of looking at and seeing the world they live in today, but my special wish for them is that they too will have a 'Maureen Potter' in their memories.

GEMMA HUSSEY

I think it wouldn't be an exaggeration to say that Maureen Potter was responsible for a lot of things that happened in my life – not least an abiding interest in theatre. People often say that politicians relish the 'roar of the greasepaint', so perhaps she played some part in an eventual political career too.

It all started because in Bray, Co. Wicklow, where I grew up, kind neighbours had an only daughter whose birthday fell on 20 January. Since I was lucky enough to be the daughter's best friend, I got to be brought to the Pantomime as part of her birthday celebrations every year for several years.

Not only that! We had the privilege of seats *in a box*, chocolates, the whole works.

Excitement about this event started to build up well before Christmas, and it didn't matter too much when Christmas was over because we had the Pantomime and Maureen Potter to look forward to.

I'll never forget the astonishment and delight of hearing Maureen Potter, after entertaining us hugely for a whole evening, looking up at our box and calling out my friend's name, and then mine. We were speechless with delight. That such a star who had danced, sung, told jokes and made us laugh so much could notice us was wonderful.

Looking back, this actually happened every year but it

seems that this did not matter: we were still transfixed with amazement each time. Never mind that she called out lots of other names (how on earth did she do it? I don't recall a list in her hand): we only heard ours.

One year, a thick fog descended on Dublin while we were inside the theatre. There was no question at all of trying to get home to Bray, so – wonder of wonders – we stayed in a hotel. I think it was the Gresham on O'Connell Street. And that year was also the year we were brought backstage after the show to meet our heroine – who laughed and rolled her eyes at the posh when we told her breathlessly we were going to stay in a hotel because of the fog.

Years and years later, after one of her impressive performances in an O'Casey play, I felt very glad to have the chance to tell her how important she had been to some small girls in Bray and to thank her.

In response, she smiled broadly and again rolled her eyes.

JOHN BEHAN

Sitting here near the river Corrib on a fine spring morning, I hear the announcement on the radio that Maureen Potter has died. The world stops and I think of the ancient Greek mariner who, when sailing past Paxos, heard a plaintive voice cry: *Great Pan is dead.*

In Irish theatrical terms, this demise closes the curtains on a great vaudeville tradition in this country, impossible to revive. I particularly remember, in the years immediately after the war, my father chugging us – my brothers and sister and me – around St Stephen's Green in a sand lorry. The excitement in the cab was palpable; we could hardly contain ourselves: we were all going to see Jimmy O'Dea and Maureen Potter in the Gaiety Pantomime.

In my Galway garden, amongst the beautiful, abundant pink blossoms on the branches of the cherry trees, there is a flurry of activity as finches and blue tits feed at the wire cages full of nuts, while Adèle King (the comedienne Twink) comes on the radio to talk to Marian Finucane about her association with the great Potter. There is grief and shock and a poignant sense of real loss in her voice. She speaks for all of us who saw or experienced the genius of Potter at work.

Now to the garden comes a beautiful bullfinch, colourful, proud and full of life, hopping along the ground, up on to a garden table and then a sudden dash into the cherry blossoms; *alive alive-o*; Maureen Potter, irrepressible, full of creative energy, dancing, singing, cracking jokes, taking us out of ourselves for a happy hour or so.

Twink speaks of Potter's great generosity in person and in spirit; how she was particularly helpful to the younger actors she influenced, especially Twink herself and Rosaleen Linehan.

As for us pantomime-goers long ago, we were starry-eyed as we got back into our sand lorry after that show. Our anticipation had been fulfilled; it had been a privilege to be entertained by such talent. Never to be forgotten. Pure magic.

If ever a person deserved a monument on the streets of Dublin it is Maureen Potter. It should be something we can all touch, tactile and human – down amongst the people at street level, representing the great tradition of Greek and Roman comedy which, through the performances of *commedia dell' arte*, lived on in the form of La Potter.

Long may her spirit live!

KEVIN REYNOLDS

On 7 April 2004, I was working down in ES1, an edit studio in the catacombs of the RTÉ Radio Centre, when I read on the 'Newstar' computer screen that Maureen Potter had passed away peacefully. We were shortly to broadcast RTÉ Radio One's arts programme, *Rattlebag*, from Prague and I was piecing together a soundscape I hoped would whet the listeners' appetite. John Banville was scheduled to read excerpts from his book *Prague Pictures* and, while I waited for him, I was editing a piece of speech I had recorded a week earlier with the playwright Tom Stoppard, who was born in the city.

When John arrived, I greeted him, shook his hand and asked him had he heard the news. There was only one piece of news that morning.

He said that he had, paraphrased Beckett, and then remarked with a sigh (which constitutes an emotional outburst for Banville) that the passing of someone who can make us laugh is truly a loss indeed.

Writers are smart guys, I thought, because it was only then I began to realise what a real loss Maureen Potter was, not only to Ireland, Europe, the World, the Universe and the Milky Way, but also to me.

Every Christmas, we were bussed from Glasnevin on the 11 or the 19A to the Gaiety Theatre. We four boys, dolled up like prize rabbits in the new Christmas clobber and under the watchful eye of my mother, arrived shining at the Pantomime. (My father, as well as living with my mother, was married to An Gárda Síochána, so he would always arrive just as the curtain was about to go up; Christmas was, and is, a busy time for those involved in The Law, but he wouldn't miss it: 'How does she think them up?')

The Gaiety Theatre, in all its gaudy splendour and plush velour seats (you had to sit upright on them to see all the action), was a wonderland of ushers and usherettes. Coats, lipstick, stockings, noise, chandeliers, boxes, famous people from television – and other youngsters who almost looked like us, yet not quite.

Southsiders.

Then the lights went down, the orchestra struck up and the words 'Hello there boys and girls' were the cue. Where are all other thoughts? *They're behind you!*

Marvel upon marvel followed. The Prince – Jimmy Bartley. The Beee-yooou-tiful Princess – Patricia Cahill. Vernon Hayden with a song, Danny Cummins as Buttons and then –

And then –

Maureen Potter.

We hung on her every move, word and gesture as she squeezed the last laugh out of us. Then, before you could catch your breath, a dance. Wow!

Then a parody of 'Medicinal Compound', and between laughs my mother was passing around the Scots Clan and Clarnico Iced Caramels, and the great thing was that Maureen Potter was loving every minute of it too!

Heaven in row H.

On the way home, endless questions. Does she have to do that again tomorrow? Is she married? Was she at home to cook Christmas dinner? Does she have little boys and girls? I thought she was like a priest in a way: she had to work at Christmas; she had a vocation and the Gaiety was her cathedral.

A few years later on one of my annual pilgrimages to the Gaeltacht (Coláiste Lurgan, Indreabhán) I met and became friendly with Seán O'Leary, Maureen Potter's son. He kindly and patiently answered all those questions with which I had plagued my mother. A celebrity-by-proxy in Connemara, he wore his mantle of received fame lightly and pleasantly.

As most mothers did, Maureen came to see her son. I wasn't there. I passionately (but secretly) wanted to meet her, but didn't manage it on that occasion.

That chance came in 1994 when the actor Johnny Murphy introduced me to 'Mo'. Awestruck, I stood in front of this diminutive, smiling woman and could only mumble. They say you should never meet your idols; they say comedians aren't funny in real life. Sometimes they're wrong. She was both funny and polite. She was herself. She was Maureen Potter and –

She called me by name.

Years later I saw her act at the Gate. My mother's eldest brother, Father P.J., has been a priest in New Zealand for the last sixty years and, as a result, our house in Glasnevin became the Unofficial New Zealand Embassy for travelling Kiwi priests and parishioners, P.J. having assured them of grub and a bed for the night. We were charged with entertaining these people so, naturally, we took them into town. On the walk home from one such excursion, a Fr Seán Hurley and I chanced our arm at ten minutes to eight and got 'returns' for *Juno and the Paycock*. Yes, *that* one: Donal McCann, John Kavanagh, Geraldine Plunkett and – Maureen Potter, holding centre stage, laughing and making us laugh in the middle of a tragedy. She seemed to be having a better time than any of us. I looked at Hurley, who was from the other end of the world, and could see he got it. He was laughing too.

Heaven in Row H.

Like most people, the last time I saw her was when she was a guest on the Abbey Theatre's centenary *Late Late Show*; I was in the audience and she was brought on during a commercial break. She was waving and smiling as always but I was struck by the toll that a lifetime of hoofing and rehearsing on bare stages and cold rehearsal rooms (is there any other kind?) had taken on her limbs and joints …

She, though, was having none of it. She came to entertain and entertain she did.

I sat there, in Row H, watching her and thinking how many times this woman had done just that – Pantos, *Juno*, *The Rising of the Moon*, Jimmy O'Dea – and here she was again. God, she was good! She could have gone anywhere – the West End, Broadway – but she chose to stay in Clontarf and entertain children of all ages. How generous! Maureen stayed true to her vocation and, like Charlie Chaplin or Stan and Olly, always made me laugh. The expression 'Old Trooper' was coined for her.

That day, 7 April 2004, my colleague Aonghus McAnally produced a lovely *Rattlebag* tribute to her. Aonghus's blood courses with show business and he knows how to do these things; Jimmy Bartley, Michael Colgan and Fred O'Donovan all contributed. Although devastated, they were great, sincere and funny, and after the programme BBC Northern Ireland asked me to send some archival material. I sent 'Christy'.

I heard him on *BBC 5 Live* that evening and smiled.

My eldest child will be four years old next Christmas. In time, she too will go to the Gaeltacht, *le cúnamh Dé*, but this Christmas we're going to the Panto. We will be in Row H.

Where will Maureen Potter be?

Look out! She's above you!

Ar dheis Dé go raibh a hanam dílis.

PART IV

The Brass

Maureen with Fred O'Donovan and Lorcan Bourke.
Courtesy of Fred O'Donovan

At the height of her career, Maureen Potter was – save for a couple of pop stars – the highest-paid entertainer in Ireland. According to impresario Fred O'Donovan, whose association with her was long and fruitful, she was a dream to deal with.

Brought up with his five brothers in Marino, only a stone's throw from Maureen Potter's Fairview, O'Donovan's theatrical career was inextricably bound up with Potter's for many, many years. 'I find it hard to remember a time working in Ireland when I wasn't working with her.'

Before producing her in Pantomime and *Gaels of Laughter* at the Gaiety, he produced and directed her show on radio (*The Maureen Potter Show*), recorded in the O'Connell Hall. This was Costume Radio. The performers did their thing in full gear in front of an audience 'which came in out of the rain'. If it was not raining and they would not come in voluntarily, Fred and his assistant would go out into the street and haul them in.

During its fourth year on air, this radio show became the highest-rated programme in the history of Radio Éireann and Fred approached Maureen Potter privately: 'You could be doing your own show at the Gaiety. I'll produce it.' But Potter, working with Jimmy O'Dea at the time, flatly refused even to consider it: '"Not while I'm working with Jimmy."

'But then Jimmy fell off his perch so I approached her again. "This is it now. You were with him until the day he died –"'

So she agreed.

Show business, however, is nothing if not pragmatic. 'We decided to call her show *Gaels of Laughter*. My thinking was that if anything happened to Maureen ... Then having a Maureen Potter show wouldn't be ...'

The son of a buyer for Hely's Office Suppliers, Fred O'Donovan himself led a pretty colourful life, even before throwing himself wholeheartedly into showbiz: for instance, he was once a graveyard sleuth for the British government.

From the time he was a small boy, he was passionately in love with aviation: his idea of a heavenly day out was to be brought to Collinstown to watch the planes and from the age of seven he haunted the Phoenix Park, where short flights in a Tiger Moth were on offer for a shilling. He became so well known to the pilots, they allowed him to collect the shillings from everyone else in the queue in return for a free ride at the end of the day.

Having dropped out of school at sixteen, he lied about his age by altering his birth certificate and was accepted by the RAF, where he was trained as a wireless operator – 'I got up to twenty-two words a minute in Morse' – and air gunner. He didn't see much action, however: 'I joined in 1944 when it was a bit of a fairyland.'

When war ended, he was selected for a specialist unit, representative of many nations, set up to search for missing airmen and war criminals. 'We had a Czech, an Englishman, an Irishman, a Scotsman, a Welshman, a French-Canadian, an Anglo-Canadian, an Australian and so on …' The unit was given a course in investigative techniques and then set out, two by two, in cars, working eighteen hours a day in all weathers and conditions.

Fred's beat was France. When he had signed on initially for the RAF, he had put on his recruitment form that he spoke two languages: 'and being English, they just assumed my Number Two language was French' when in fact it was Irish. And so he was dispatched to France, where he 'travelled the length and breadth' without a word of the language. But he and his mate did fulfil their mission, foraging through remote cemeteries and presiding over the exhumation of bodies for repatriation. 'Unfortunately, I caught TB from the corpses.'

He wasn't the only one to contract the disease and the RAF sent them all to a sanatorium in Davos, Switzerland.

The conventional wisdom about the treatment of TB in those days was that the patient had to lie absolutely still: 'You weren't supposed to move even your toes.' Once, Fred woke at high noon to the sight of a circle of earnest faces around his bed. 'This man will cure himself,' said the Head Honcho to his underlings, 'he sleeps all the time.' And indeed, from the medics' perspective, he and his five confrères seemed to be model patients, lying quietly in their beds all day.

Night-time was different.

Ten p.m. Moonlight sparking on frozen snow. All peaceful in the san. But like wraiths in a Hammer Horror graveyard, six figures are rising stealthily from their beds. Each night they climb through a window then scrunch, on foot, three miles to the nearest town. There they go to the nightclub, they smoke, they drink, they dance, they drink again.

They then scrunch three miles back to the hospital through temperatures usually in the region of twenty-below. They get back in the way they had come out and are sleeping peacefully by five a.m.

'Well, it was the only way to live. A lot of the people there were from Dachau and Belsen and you knew they had no chance at all. So you had to enjoy yourself.' In fact, one of the gang, a submarine commander 'and always pickled', had been given less than six months to live. Many, many years later, Fred O'Donovan ran into him, very much alive, propping up the bar of a Dublin hotel, 'and still pickled'.

Interviewed in his gorgeous house on the heights above Howth village, where there is a view of the sea from every room and even from the front door, O'Donovan is surrounded by Potter and general theatrical memorabilia. No longer in rude health, he fires up when talking about her. 'The name "Maureen Potter" is synonymous with genius. She succeeded in doing what no other person has ever done here, as far as I am aware. When you talk about her as a dancer, you discover she's a singer; when you talk about her as a singer, she's an actor; as an actor, she's the greatest comedienne Ireland has ever produced – all these combined talents – pure magic!

'I'll give you an example. I was bringing Jack Benny to Ireland, but out of the blue, he rang me: "I'm going to England so I'd like to drop in on the way and see this Gaiety Theatre of yours –" He was a real pro. Sussing everything out in advance.

'Well, as it happened, he arrived during Panto time. We were absolutely packed so I said: "Jack, you'll have to stand at the back. We have no seats."

'"No problem," he said, "I'll look at the first act."

'Well, he watched the first act and then he turned to me at the interval and he said: "Why do you want me here at all? That lady is the best talent I have ever seen in my life. I'd be afraid to come here now." So now I had to persuade him that his was a different talent ...'

In O'Donovan's (experienced) opinion, a lot of comedians are boring people off-stage, but Potter was not. She was as hilarious in the green room as on the stage.

Did she never have an 'off' day?

'Well, if she did, I never saw it. I never saw her depressed.'

Since his family and hers holidayed together when both

sets of children were small, Fred is probably one of the few people who had an opportunity to observe (not know) the 'real' Maureen. They liked Kelly's Hotel in Rosslare; and once they all travelled just a few miles north of where they lived to Portmarnock Country Club, where he was part owner. 'And what most people don't realise is that Jack, her husband, is great company, a very humorous man. People who didn't know him thought he was dour – he was known as "rattle the keys" because he'd come in to collect her after the show and he'd rattle the keys. He was just being protective.

'That holiday in Portmarnock was the best holiday we ever had. She walked with Sally [Fred's wife]. Jack and I played football with the kids, and Mrs Brennan, the woman she brought with her to look after her kids and who *adored* Maureen, bullied the kitchen staff into giving Maureen's kids the best of everything at the children's tea. The hell with our kids. The hell with everyone's kids but Maureen's.

'She was Maureen's second bodyguard. She had a lot of malapropisms, though, and I think that's where Maureen might have got some of her material. For instance, I had formed a little trio from the Young Dublin Singers, and we called them Maxi, Dick and Twink. Maureen loved them, so of course Mrs Brennan loved them too. "I heard them again today on the wireless: that Maxi, Dick and Prick."'

Yet, despite the holidays, like most people who worked with her, Fred finds it very difficult to describe the 'real' Maureen Potter and can do so only in the most general terms. He is not being evasive. He is simply stuck. 'It's hard to explain. She was just great company. She was relaxed when she was off-stage. I suppose that's the best way you could describe it.'

Word spread about Potter through the English impresarios, 'because you see there were few shows in England that succeeded during the summer – only Blackpool. Even the Palladium wasn't doing well. They made her all sorts of offers, even the variety lead in the Palladium. I couldn't get involved because, naturally, my interest was to keep her so I told her she had to make her own decision.

'She got offers from America too. I had produced a TV show for Ed Sullivan, mostly singers, people like Liam Devally, but she was in it doing a sketch as a baby in a cot. The Americans went wild about her –'

She turned everyone down.

She never had an agent 'and I never signed a contract with Maureen; never had a cross word about anything to do with business. With regard to money, she was a partner, inasmuch as when we paid all the expenses, she got more or less a dividend, not a salary or fee.'

They did argue about scripts. 'Comics are inclined to grab a script: "Yeah, this is it" – but I'm there as an observer. I'm the audience and if it *isn't* "it" I have to be truthful. So they'd all adjourn to Sinnott's to call me all sorts of a bastard and then they'd come back and say, "You were right!"'

Unlike Hal Roach elsewhere in this book, Fred O'Donovan believes that had she taken up the American offers, she could have made a lot of money. On the other hand, 'She did well in Ireland. She was one of the best-paid artistes here – although maybe a couple of pop singers made more.'

Over the years, stories have persisted in the theatrical undergrowth about Maureen · Potter's predilection for insisting on cutting any gag or line that got a bigger laugh than hers. O'Donovan hotly disputes this. 'That is not true. That might have been true of Jimmy O'Dea – but I'm only going on hearsay there. With her, I *know* it was on the contrary. She encouraged people. And if you tried to top her, next night she'd come back with a funnier line because she'd probably gone home and beat Jack's head off the wall: "He got a big laugh on that, I want a bigger laugh –"'

'It would be far more likely I would do that than she would do it. If she was getting no laughs, it'd be me who'd cut the script because she was the star of the show.'

The only episode of 'script grabbing' he can remember is not even a script. 'There was a song that I wanted the Leddy

Sisters to sing, but when Maureen heard it, she said: "I'd like that." So I went to the Leddy Sisters and told them Maureen had taken a shine to the song. They just laughed and said: "Well, we weren't all that mad about it anyway.' That song was 'Send in the Clowns', and with it, he tried a thing that hadn't been done before in variety here. He opened the show with it: a spot slowly travelling up to the top of a ladder, revealing his star seated on its apex. 'That was the thing with her. If I asked any British or American artist to open like that, they wouldn't, not with people still coming in. It's common now, of course, but in those days you put in fifteen minutes before you even caught a glimpse of the star.'

Maureen, Hal Roach and Stephen Brennan.
Photo: James D. O'Callaghan

One of the shows was in full rehearsal one sunny afternoon when a breathless detective came running into the theatre to inform them that a warning had been received:

they all had fifteen minutes to leave the theatre. The IRA had placed a bomb on the premises.

'Did they give a code word?' Fred was suspicious.

But yes, the code word had been given and recognised.

Quickly, everyone in the theatre gathered up his or her belongings and repaired to St Stephen's Green across the road. 'Well, it was a lovely day. We had to continue rehearsing if there was going to be a theatre to come back to.

'We were just going in through the main gates of the Green when Maureen stopped dead. "Fred! I left all me scripts in Number One!"

'I ran back to the theatre and was just going in through the door when I looked at my watch. Right on fifteen minutes.'

He hesitated. Torn. Maureen losing her scripts versus being blown up by the IRA. Which was the worst?

He opted to get the scripts.

JOE DOWLING

The name Maureen Potter automatically brings a smile to everyone's lips. Even those who never met her had the sense that she was an old friend who always gave them a laugh. It was that familiarity and warmth that made her beloved by successive generations of Irish audiences.

I first fell in love with her as a small child getting my first taste of theatre and, many years later, when I had the privilege of working with her, she turned out to be as warm and as loveable as I had always imagined. Maureen (for the first name was enough to identify her) was the Queen of Irish comedy for a very long time and the monarchy ended with her. She was unique and cannot be replaced, no matter how hard the pretenders try. She was also the last link with a world of Variety theatre that once flourished in cities and towns around the country but which lost its lustre with the rise of television. The actor who, on his deathbed, declared that 'dying is easy, comedy is hard' spoke a truth recognised by anyone who has tried to make an audience laugh for a whole evening. Maureen did just that for over sixty years and she reinvented herself and her talent to reflect different times in her own life.

For a star-struck child growing up in Dublin in the late fifties, there was no greater treat than the annual visit to the Gaiety Pantomime. From September on, I longed for the shortening of the days and the onset of winter weather that would bring the special day. The opening scene was invariably set on a village green somewhere in 'fairytale land'. It was a place of painted glory where the sun always shone. A group of sturdy peasants greeted the morning with a song and a dance but, for all the attention we paid, they might as well not have bothered. The chatter of the audience only diminished with the arrival of our favourites. The stars made their entrances in order of their billing. First came Vernon Hayden. For years, as the fiendish villain of the piece, he was the implacable enemy of several generations of young Dubliners. Oh, how we loved to hiss and boo that most gentle of men. Then, with panache and swagger, the principal boy arrived, usually played by a long and leggy Hazel Yeomans. How many pre-adolescent pulses beat stronger at her arrival? Then her princess, played with a gentle charm by Ursula Doyle.

But the moment we all waited for was the procession of the comics. Danny Cummins first, a small mischievous imp of a man with the face of a bold child, then Maureen, equally tiny but huge in her warmth, her energy and her powerful connection to the whole audience …

But all this was a prelude to the moment that defined the whole experience. The arrival of Jimmy O'Dea, the greatest dame of all time and whose large brown eyes could, with the slightest twinkle, cause hysteria among the thousand or so packed into the Gaiety. Even at a remove of nearly half a century, I can still experience the excitement and the breathtaking delight I felt at the sight of this diminutive genius dressed as a woman in a ridiculous outfit. The magic of theatre manages to turn dross into gold. In Jimmy's case, gold was already there. He just made it even brighter.

Once they were all on, then the fun got going. Scene would follow scene in rapid succession. Goldilocks would meet her three bears, Aladdin would rub his lamp, Cinderella would go to the ball and midnight would find her wanting. The plots never mattered because we already knew the outcome. What mattered were the familiar routines. The chase that would end in serious slapstick, the villain coming up behind Maureen and Jimmy to the ear-shattering sound of an audience determined to give fair warning. 'Look behind you,' we would roar in unison, always hoping that our pleas would be ignored. We talked our way through the soppy bits where the prince and princess, both played by women, would sing of their undying love. The deeper implications of this same-sex display of affection were a matter of total indifference to us. We laughed along at the incomprehensible political satire, added so that our parents would not be too bored.

The bit I loved the most and imitated at home throughout the year was the final walk down. Once the problems had all been solved and the wrongs righted, everyone would depart for the palace and reappear in new and even more sparkling outfits. Again an order of precedence was observed until Maureen and Jimmy would make their final appearances, usually with outrageous headdresses and gowns of sumptuous splendour. The final goodbyes were offered and we were on our way home to dream of the next year and counting the days until the magic could be recreated.

When Jimmy died in 1964, the obituaries insisted that it was the end of an era and probably the end of the Gaiety Theatre, where he had reigned supreme for thirty years. Nobody really reckoned on the diminutive ball of energy, his loyal number two for so long, taking the top spot and making it her own. But before long, with the encouragement and writing skills of her husband, Jack O'Leary, and the producing and marketing skills of Fred O'Donovan, Mo Potter became the unchallenged star of both summer and Christmas in South King Street. Her career had come a long way since her childhood beginning as one of 'The Two Maureens' – the second being Maureen Flanagan, a name familiar these days only to fans in what are euphemistically called their 'twilight years' and, of course, the faithful in the business.

Her brush with history when she played before Hitler has been well documented and, indeed, was one of Maureen's favourite anecdotes. Her return home at the outbreak of war in 1939 ended the potential for an international career but began a love affair with Irish audiences that lasted until her death.

Her partnership with O'Dea covered twenty years and defined Dublin comedy for several generations. With Jimmy as Mrs Mulligan, the pride of the Coombe, and Maureen as Auntie Ginnie, who was fond of a jar and could always be persuaded to sing at a party, they created a pair of characters who defined an age and a city with the same attention to detail that Sean O'Casey had done a generation before. Mrs Mulligan was as prototypical of her native city as Joxer Daly or Maisie Madigan. O'Dea and his writer, Harry O'Donovan, drew from the same music-hall tradition that had inspired much of O'Casey's comedy. In the south-side elegance of South King Street, O'Dea and Potter combined to shock middle-class audiences with their ribald humour. It is hard to remember now that Jimmy O'Dea was widely regarded as a vulgar comedian whom respectable people should avoid. But, true to the Irish spirit, such advice was ignored by the majority and both he and Maureen became household names.

Following Jimmy's death, Maureen made the Gaiety her kingdom and those years were golden ones for her. Every Christmas, she headlined the Panto and, come the summer, she was back with yet another *Gaels of Laughter*. She was one of the few Irish artists whose name on the marquee could fill the house. People from all walks of life and from all around the country became devotees. Her television shows were hugely popular.

There was no end to the adulation. Rosaleen Linehan, herself no mean comedienne, described Maureen as the most talented person she ever worked with. In a recent conversation, Milo O'Shea, a legendary figure in Irish theatre, told me of Maureen's gift for helping others to shape a laugh and of her kindness, especially to children. Within her profession, she was loved and revered as no other I have ever known.

The physical toll taken by her incredible schedule was immense. Knee replacements, arthritis and stomach complaints meant that the high-octane energy of the Gaiety shows had to slow down. Rather than go into some gentle retirement, however, Mo once again reinvented herself and resumed her career as a fine character actor on the legitimate stage. This was where I played a small part in her amazing story.

I left the Abbey in 1985 in a flurry of controversy. Michael Colgan, recently appointed as director of the Gate Theatre, gave me shelter at Cavendish Row, asking me what plays I wanted to do there. Among the titles I suggested was O'Casey's civil-war masterpiece *Juno and the Paycock*. I wanted to direct that quintessentially Abbey play at the Gate for many reasons. I had done a production of it for the Abbey's seventy-fifth anniversary in 1979. Starring Siobhán McKenna and Philip O'Flynn, it was weighted down with tradition and with echoes of other productions. I had been deeply disappointed in the results and longed to do it in a smaller theatre. I wanted to do it with a cast who had never done the roles before. I also really wanted to see Donal McCann play Captain Boyle. McCann was at the height of his formidable powers as an actor but he had never played the great O'Casey roles. It seemed ideal to match him and the play at the Gate. Michael Colgan and I started to find the cast to surround him. Maureen was an obvious and perfect choice for Maisie Madigan, the noisy neighbour whose appearance at the party in Act Two is one of the highlights of the play.

She had stopped doing *Gaels of Laughter* and had not yet found her new artistic home in Clontarf Castle. It was a special treat for me to have her in the cast. I had known Maureen socially while I was in the Abbey, but because of my childhood adoration and my awe at her talent, I had always felt shy in her company.

The first day of rehearsal for *Juno* was really the first time we properly met. I was anxious about the new production and it took a while to realise that Maureen was as shy with me as I was with her. She was nervous that people from the 'legitimate' theatre would look down on mere 'variety artistes'. She also feared that we would be deeply intellectual and analytical about the work. Indeed, her worst fears seemed to be realised because, as with all plays, the first few days were spent around a table discussing the work. We spent hours every day analysing the characters, the language and O'Casey's intentions. Maureen would sit there, seemingly involved and engaged. Later she admitted that, in the evenings, she would complain to her husband, Jack: 'Janey, all they do is *talk*. When are they ever going to get up and *do* it?'

Once we started to rehearse properly, her contributions were magnificent. She knew the character without any need for literary or psychological analysis. From her first entrance she galvanised the action and was a powerful and hilarious force that kept the play going. The party scene, which is broken up by the arrival of Mrs Tancred grieving for her son, has never been better played. Maureen, together with Geraldine Plunkett as Juno, John Kavanagh as Joxer and Donal McCann as the Captain, played it to the hilt.

Maureen (Maisie Madigan) with Donal McCann in
Juno and the Paycock. Photo: Tom Lawlor

We added extra lines and remarks that were entirely in the spirit of the text. Called upon to sing, Maisie Madigan obliges with a high-pitched hilarious rendition of 'If I Were a

Blackbird'. I decided that, if Maureen Potter was at a party, one song would never be enough. It certainly would not be enough for the audience. So we added a second song. I asked Maureen for a suggestion – knowing that she would come up with exactly the right number for the occasion. Without even hesitating, she immediately began to sing:

> Smile awhile and kiss me, say adieu
> When the clouds roll by, I'll come to you ...

She continued with the song as the other actors joined in and the party was in full swing.

We kept it in and, during the course of that long-running production, every Maisie that followed her also sang that song.

Her comic skills came as no surprise. However, it was in the third act that she showed the extent of her acting ability. When Maisie arrives to tell Juno of the death of her son – murdered as a reprisal for the killing of Robbie Tancred – there is a scene of real anguish and heartbreak as a mother hears the dreaded news of her beloved son's death. Maureen Potter played that scene with absolute stillness and integrity. There was no hint of the comic genius; there was no playing to the audience. She was brilliantly in character and the hard-bitten Maisie Madigan was filled with distress and sympathy for Juno's plight. It was acting of the highest order and it banished any suspicion that Maureen was 'only' a variety artist.

The success of that production brought us to many exciting places and finally to Broadway. It was Maureen's first time in New York and, like the rest of us, she was excited to play on the Great White Way. The tragedy was that, by that time, the agonising pain in her knees meant that she spent all her time off-stage lying on the flat of her back in great pain. What was remarkable was that, in spite of her sufferings, on stage she was transformed and never missed a beat. She sang and danced and acted her heart out. Once off the stage, the agony would resume. 'Dr Theatre,' she would laugh, 'cures you every time'; so, in spite of her own personal distress, she was the life and soul of that company and, of course, audiences in New York were as crazy about her as they had been everywhere else.

The only appearance Maureen made at the Abbey Theatre was in Hugh Leonard's play *Moving*, which we did together in the early nineties. The part was tailor-made for her and the experience was a happy one.

Early in rehearsal, the management told us that Lord Snowdon would be visiting us the next day to take some photographs for an article to be printed in the *Sunday Telegraph*. It is not a normal part of a rehearsal process to entertain royalty and we were all a little stiff when the distinguished visitor arrived. The morning session was artificial and strained. After a little lunch accompanied by a glass of wine, Maureen returned, determined to break the ice. No sooner had his Lordship set up his camera again than she broke into a deliciously filthy rhyme she had learnt from Jimmy O'Dea. The silence that followed seemed to go on forever. It was broken by the sound of a rumbling and long-lasting royal laugh and, from then on, the photos got better and the aristocratic reserve broke down.

Maureen Potter could have been an international star. She had the vitality, the charm, the skills as a dancer and singer and that wonderful ability to make us laugh at ourselves. She had many offers and she declined them all. She chose to stay at home because her family came first and because she loved the Irish audiences who offered her devotion in return. She also loved the Gaiety Theatre, her second home. Generations of Dubliners remember with great fondness how she introduced them to the joys of live theatre. I am among them. I feel honoured to have been a small part of that great journey. God bless you, Mo. You will never be forgotten.

MARTIN FAHY

During my childhood, Christmas time was Panto time in our family household. Annually my parents, two sisters and I attended the matinée performance at the Gaiety on St Stephen's Day. Because there were no previews in those days, this matinée performance was actually the first run of the show in front of a paying audience, the significance of which did not occur to me until I joined the Abbey Theatre in the early 1970s.

Attendance at the performance necessitated an early lunch – usually the remains of the turkey and ham from the Christmas dinner – so we could be in town before one o'clock to join an already large queue.

We queued for over two hours before curtain up.

Was there no advance booking system in the 1950s? It certainly would have saved me all the anxiety I experienced worrying that the 'House Full' sign would be placed ahead of our position! It never happened, however, and for many years on a St Stephen's afternoon I sat in the Gaiety, mesmerised by Maureen and her fellow artistes.

These childhood memories came flooding back when, in early 1992, I was told by Garry Hynes, at that time the artistic director of the Abbey Theatre, that Maureen Potter had been invited to play Mary Quirke in the forthcoming production of *Moving* by Hugh Leonard. I greeted the news with a mixture of excitement, even thrill, tinged with a little anxiety.

Excited that I would have the opportunity to meet a childhood heroine.

Thrilled that a play by Hugh Leonard, directed by Joe Dowling and with a cast that already included John Kavanagh, Johnny Murphy, Anita Reeves, Marion O'Dwyer, John Olohan and now Maureen Potter, would certainly draw large attendances and keep the theatre's finances in order.

However, I was anxious because, given Maureen's status in the entertainment world, as opposed to the modest level of the Abbey's salaries, I might be unable to close the deal and bring her on board.

I need not have worried; Maureen graciously accepted the going rate and joined the company for the production.

This was the star's only appearance in a production at the Abbey. The play was a resounding success and drew capacity attendances for its run.

Maureen in Moving by Hugh Leonard. Photo: Tom Lawlor

In the course of it, Maureen continually informed me of her delight to be performing in the Abbey and how kind the staff were to her. (Perhaps the staff did pay extra attention to her – in my view, their way of paying tribute to one of our greatest entertainers.)

During my time as general manager of the Abbey, it was my practice to attend the last performance of each play to express thanks to the artistes for participating in the production. It was a particular joy to have had the opportunity to thank Maureen, not only for performing at the Abbey, but also for the wonderful enjoyment she gave me over the years.

When it came to consideration of herself as a bona fide actor, Mo Potter was self-effacing. I remember offering her a role in an Abbey production and, in charmingly turning it down, there was much mock horror at the notion of, as she put it, 'going legit', of sharing the stage with Abbey actors, indeed of the very notion that she might be considered an 'ac-tore'. I can still hear her say that 'ac-tore', her mouth forming an amused 'o' on the second syllable. She subsequently did appear at the Abbey, just the wanst, and several times at the Gate and the Gaiety in what is rather ridiculously referred to as 'legitimate theatre'. And, of course, she proved effortlessly to be the real thing, the genuine article, the johnnymagory. But it was in the 'illegitimate theatre' of Pantomime and variety that she made her name and won for herself a very special place in the hearts of Irish people everywhere. I was a child during the heyday of the Maureen Potter reign at the Gaiety. My parents would bring us on special Christmas trips to Dublin which would include a visit to the zoo, to our aunts in Terenure and to the Gaiety Panto. Like many people of my generation, Maureen Potter is woven into the fabric of our golden childhoods. That is her tilt at immortality, her priceless legacy. She had two sovereign, mysterious gifts: the gift of stage presence and the gift of inspiring laughter. Both of these gifts were honed by an immaculate technique forged in the rough and tumble world of her chosen craft. Personally I only knew her slightly but I remember her as charming, witty, attentive, big-hearted, humble, life-affirming. I am sure, like all of us, she had her faults but the gods will always forgive those who can make them laugh. That ability to inspire laughter was her enviable trademark. 'The Gael of Laughter' might serve as her epitaph.

JOHN McCOLGAN

I first saw Maureen Potter in a Gaiety Panto in 1960. It was the beginning of a life-long fascination with and an admiration for this multi-talented lady who, by the sheer energy, honesty and power of her stage presence, left an indelible impression on her audiences. During the following years I saw Maureen every chance I got – on Sunday afternoons in *The Maureen Potter Show* for Radio Éireann at the O'Connell Hall, in countless Christmas Pantos and at the summer *Gaels of Laughter* at the Gaiety. During the 1970s and 1980s I had the privilege and pleasure of working with Maureen on numerous television specials for RTÉ. Four years later I produced and directed *Super Trouper*, a biographical television documentary on Maureen and I also produced a video of her wonderful one-woman show at Clontarf Castle.

Over the years my affection and admiration for her grew. Every project with Maureen was fun, as one savoured again her delicious sense of irony and her wicked, self-mocking sense of humour. And, of course, she was always aided and abetted by her stoic scriptwriter, sometimes personal manager and husband of thirty years, the Quiet Man, Captain Jack O'Leary.

John McColgan with Maureen. Courtesy of Abhann

On 18 January 1999 I produced a celebration concert to honour Maureen in the Gaiety Theatre. With Her Excellency President Mary McAleese in attendance, many of Maureen's colleagues and friends in the entertainment industry performed on stage in that special night of tribute to Maureen. At the end of the evening, top of the bill of course, Maureen received a ten-minute standing ovation from those present. The frail figure in the spotlight, who had enriched the lives of five generations, was taking her final bow on the stage of her beloved Gaiety. It was a moment when all of us who were there wanted to express our love and gratitude to a great lady, a unique artiste, an Irish icon, a Super Trouper.

We won't see the likes of you again – we love you Maureen!

BRÍD DUKES

Soon after the opening of the Belltable Arts Centre, one of the exciting rumours I recall was the possibility that *The Maureen Potter Show* was going out on tour. It became a reality in June 1983. The deal was that the Belltable would supply the first half of the entertainment and that with her pal and permanent sidekick, Thelma Ramsey, as piano accompanist, Maureen would play the second half.

On 6 June I was at the box-office when she came through the door. I heard her before I saw her and, not having met her before, I was thrown. I had not anticipated her minuteness, her large glasses or her larger minder. Jack seemed enormous but while Maureen was tiny she filled the space. She reminded me of my first encounter with my maternal grandmother on the platform at Westland Row station years before. Both women were diminutive and possessed of amazingly expressive eyes that communicated vulnerability, hesitancy and a wish for acceptance and to please. My immediate response was a desire to cuddle her, but she was whisked away backstage while Jack and I sorted out the business details of the run.

Each night, from my position at the back of the Belltable's balcony, I was overwhelmed by the on-stage energy and sparkle which belied the physical frailty of this small woman.

She sang and danced like a young one at an all-Ireland *fleadh*; this was showmanship and professionalism at its most complete.

Some two and a half thousand people saw her show that week, and having done so, I am sure that all of them feel as grateful and privileged, as I do.

PHYLLIS RYAN

There was one period in my life in theatre that I can truly say was one of the most rewarding, and that was when I came very close to really knowing Maureen Potter.

Knowing how much she and Siobhán McKenna admired each other and how close they were in friendship, I longed to find a show that would bring them together and, also, that I might have some place in such an adventure via my company, Gemini Productions. This dream came true due to a revival I saw of the film *Arsenic and Old Lace*, which sent hilarious images rocking around my brain: my two great ladies performing the charitable act of assisting lonely old gentlemen into a better world (the next) by putting arsenic in their elderberry wine.

Not surprisingly, both ladies jumped at the opportunity, because Siobhán was always moaning and ullagóning to me about never being cast in comedy – 'they never cast me as anything except one of these Drama Queens' – and I knew Maureen would love to try her hand at 'legitimate' theatre. (Incredibly, Maureen, the artist, had so much humility in her nature that she lacked any real sense of her own greatness and believed that actors who worked in serious drama, outside that other world of variety, had far superior gifts to her own. This is invariably true of those few who are specially chosen, trusted with that extra grace that transforms the good into the great.)

And so the play was produced at the Gaiety during the Dublin Theatre Festival, aided and abetted by that great showman Fred O'Donovan and the then festival director

Lewis Clohessy. It was, of course, an instant and brilliant success, with a wonderful supporting cast and stylish direction by William H. Chappell. During the rehearsals and run of this play, there was a rare sense of unity in the company – a sharing in each other's problems and achievements, with everyone being on equal terms, despite the presence of our two great 'stars', who pulled no rank and sought no privileges. There was great happiness in that company, and that spirit resulted in a superb show, beautiful to behold and hard to follow.

And Maureen and Siobhán and Phyllis were close, united in grief when we lost that lovable actor Liam Sweeney, and also in joy because the dream had been a good one and we had brought it to such a successful reality.

Maureen Potter embodied Pantomime to me and my children, to my colleagues in theatre and to everyone who ever entered into the shimmering world of magic that was the Christmas season. Again, in the *Gaels of Laughter* shows, which brightened our doubtful summers, she bestowed on all manner of people the freedom to laugh, to let go, to have fun, even those who were depressed, grieving or sick in mind or body.

She was fun to be with when I met her relaxing after a show or at some social event where her wit held us enthralled – never unkind, never undermining her targets, but spot on in observation and mimicry.

Of course I was in awe of her, mainly because I knew no one else who was so multi-talented or who had worked and honed each separate ability so assiduously until near-perfection was achieved in each.

Maureen could dance, sing, act and clown brilliantly and beautifully. She could also join our world of drama and, as well as playing Abby in *Arsenic and Old Lace*, could bring her rich gift of characterisation to such roles as Maisie Madigan in O'Casey's *Juno and the Paycock*.

She was in remarkably good spirits when we last met at the end of the *Late Late Show* honouring a hundred years of the Abbey Theatre. She told me how glad she was to see me and so many of her old mates again. 'Are you going to the party?' I said I was and she grumbled a bit: 'I have to go *home*' – rather like a bold child. Then she said goodbye and her devoted, ever-watchful husband, Jack, brought her home.

When she died, there was such a general sense of bereavement, such an overwhelming sense of loss that the streets seemed to throb with a common grief. It was a personal matter to the people of Dublin, who moved more heavily along the suitably grey, rain-soaked pavements than before the news broke. On radio, TV and in the newspapers, journalists battled to find the words, the phrases, that would convey even a fraction of the genius of this tiny Dublin lady. There were accolades from the humblest in the land and from the greatest, from rich and poor people. And there were tears from people who just loved her, who didn't give a button what gifts she had, but knew who she was and where she came from.

At her Removal (that word is so strange) I heard all the echoes of things said and written before, about how the world will be poorer now and how there will never be anyone like her and how this is the end of an era. And I thought: is this all we can do? Keep saying the same old things to comfort each other – because the familiar sometimes brings ease?

But when I came home that evening and was alone, I thought how true it is that the world is now a poorer place – and that, indeed, we will not see her like again.

Because, even when she had retired due to ill health and we didn't see her, we knew she was still a living presence; she, who had brightened our youth and our ageing, who had taught us how to receive the precious gift of laughter, who had known the darkest days, had continued onwards and upwards, bringing relief and assurance to the lives of countless others.

No, there will *not* be another like her. It *is* the end of an era and the world – a poor enough place as it stands – will feel emptier and we will be left to wonder if we 'appreciated' enough all that she was and did for us and if we loved her enough and if we were truly thankful.

FERGUS BOURKE

Maureen and Siobhan McKenna in Arsenic and Old Lace at the Gaiety. Photo: Fergus Bourke

I had the privilege of photographing the two *grandes dames* of Irish theatre: Siobhán McKenna and Maureen Potter, two great professionals and two great friends, as they appeared as Abby and Martha in *Arsenic and Old Lace* (Gaiety Theatre, 1985); the chemistry created on stage by these great actresses is what the magic of live theatre is all about.

PART V

On stage

After working together in Arsenic and Old Lace, *Maureen Potter and Siobhán McKenna kept in constant touch. 'She used to telephone me from the Druid in Galway,' said Potter, 'and say: "Oh God I wish I was back in the Gaiety in* Arsenic.*"'*

They were in separate hospitals on the night before McKenna died. From her bed in the Blackrock Clinic, Siobhán sent a bottle of champagne to Maureen's bed in Baggot Street Hospital. The card with it read: 'I hope we'll be doing Arsenic *again.'*

Virtually all of the actors who worked with Maureen Potter on stage, in radio or in film have nothing but good things to say about her (allowing for the fact that she was such a stickler for hard work and accuracy!)

Jonathan Ryan was lucky enough to find himself working in that famous production of Arsenic. *First, however, he served a (short) apprenticeship with Potter in Panto.*

JONATHAN RYAN

To anyone who grew up in Dublin in the fifties and sixties, Maureen Potter was firstly the funny, bouncy lady roaring '*Chrissstee!*' in the Gaiety Pantos, and then Ag-enn-es shouting for '*Jeh-ehm!*' on Radio Éireann. In both, in all her personae, she was larger than life.

As for me, I never dreamt when growing up that one day I'd be up on that stage *with* her!

When I first approached Irish Actors Equity regarding 'wanting to be an actor', the then general secretary, Dermot Doolan, looked kindly at me: 'So you want to be an actor? Well, go up to the Gaiety and see Ursula Doyle and see if she has anything for you in the Panto, and if she does, come back to me in three months' time and we'll see if you still want to be an actor!' I had no idea what he meant.

But that Christmas 1977, Ursula Doyle did give muggins a gig as Second Woodsman from the Left in *Little Red Riding Hood*, with Maureen Potter starring above the title, and also Danny Cummins, Cecil Nash, Vernon Hayden, Johnny Logan, Catherine Byrne, Paddy Dawson and Deborah Pearce.

Variety! Another world! My introduction to people born and bred to it!

In this '*thee-ayter*' as he used to call it, Cecil Nash, for instance, was a delight, a joy, a throw-back to the days of 'the fit-ups' (touring shows, usually, but not always under canvas); Vernon Hayden, playing his usual role of villain, was another real pro and a true gentleman; Danny Cummins was hilarious, creative and generous.

Ursula Doyle and Maureen were very close – that much was instantly clear from the first, fascinating rehearsal; what was also clear was that Maureen was very much in control of things. She got most of the funny lines, even those originally given to (or ad libbed) by others. She was the star, that was the way things worked and, although I heard the odd grumble, everyone accepted it.

As the rookie, I used to stand in the wings and marvel at the skill she displayed in her solo pieces. Her total command of the stage, her sheer enjoyment of being out there on her own with the audience in the palm of her hand, was mesmerising. Needless to say, she noticed me lurking in the shadows (she couldn't have missed me!) and one evening asked me why I was there. I told her I was simply watching and admiring and then dared to ask her how it felt to be 'out there on your own'. Her reply was simple: 'Someday,' she said, 'maybe you'll know what it's like!'

As it happened I found out just two days after the panto closed on 4 March.

During the run of *Red Riding Hood*, I learned that the Rathmines and Rathgar Musical Society was looking for a young man to play Gaston, the male juvenile lead in *Gigi* – opening 6 March.

Having auditioned and been offered the part, it transpired that the R&R rehearsed only on weekday evenings. So if I were to play the part, I would have to be released by the Gaiety.

Gigi was a great 'shop window' opportunity for me, an unknown, to play a major role in a big show – and as the

R&R had such an excellent relationship with producer Fred O'Donovan, and everyone at the Gaiety, the powers-that-be in the society did not anticipate any problems getting me released after my one tiny Panto scene: the 'Doctor Cure-All' sketch (during which Danny used to really wind Maureen up with his ad libbing), which was over and done with by about 8.20 every evening. So, no problem. I could be at *Gigi* rehearsals by 8.30.

Well – no.

Fred O'Donovan was away in the US so Maureen's brother, Jimmy Potter, was deputising for him. Release Ryan? You must be joking. He just didn't want to know.

But after much to-ing and fro-ing, impassioned pleading from me and kind interventions on my behalf by Vernon Hayden and Danny Cummins – both of whom recognised what an opportunity it was for 'the young fella', as they called me – a strange compromise was reached. I would perform the sketch and then go up to Rathmines – on three nights out of the five. On the other two evenings, I was required to sit in the dressing room from 8.20 until nearly 11 o'clock, so I could briefly appear at the back of the curtain call.

That's showbiz!

I had been told, by the way, that Maureen had agreed to the semi-release and, three or four nights into the run of *Gigi*, there I was, centre stage, right in the middle of singing the title song of the show, when whom did I see standing in the exact same spot in the wings *I* used to occupy watching *her*? You guessed it! Mo Po.

And in the green room after the show she came up to me: '*Now* you know!'

Some years later, in the 1985 Theatre Festival, I was to work with her again. She and Siobhán McKenna were cast as Martha and Abby, the Brewster sisters, in *Arsenic and Old Lace* at the Gaiety, with Garrett Keogh, Kevin Flood, Maurie Taylor, Des Nealon, Gerry Alexander, Liz Lloyd – and myself as Mortimer Brewster. It was the first time these two female powerhouses had ever worked together and much was made in the newspapers of 'the *grande dame* of the Irish theatre' and 'the queen of Irish comedy' coming together. So much so that the show sold out on day one.

If my introduction to acting through Panto was fascinating, this was doubly so because now I had the privilege of seeing, not only the skill of *two* great actresses, but also the enormous respect, not to speak of the obvious affection, each had for the other. This was a pairing made in heaven and watching them in rehearsal was a joy, often hilarious. On the one hand was Maureen's instinctive sense of comedy (so much of it in her physical awareness and stagecraft, her sense of her own physical appearance), on the other, Siobhán's stateliness and dramatic 'nous'. I had several scenes with just the two of them and was often hard put not to laugh, even during the run!

In rehearsal, for instance, Siobhán would frequently pause and very slowly look behind her to see what Maureen was 'up to' back there. She had every reason to check because Mo had worked out all sorts and bits of 'business' that involved her almost hiding behind Siobhán or tiptoeing around her like a little satellite.

Siobhán had done her homework on the actors with whom she'd never previously worked, including me, and having been told that I was a bit of an impressionist, marked my cards early in the rehearsal period: 'Now I hope we won't be getting any Cary Grant impersonations, Jonathan?'

'Perish the thought!' says I. 'Besides, he's very difficult to do.'

Fine.

I was a *good* boy.

We were about half-way through the run when, at a point in the play where Martha and Abby, all dressed up in black lace, are about to go down to tell the police everything (while simultaneously planning to poison a judge) *it happened.*

As Mortimer, I was upstage of the two actresses, at the top of the stairs, desperately trying to stop them leaving. I looked down and, to my absolute amazement, there they were, the *grande dame* of the Irish theatre and the queen of

Irish comedy, both with their backs to the audience, pulling faces, gurning up at me for all they were worth. I had experienced this phenomenon before in a semi-professional production, but *this* was in front of nearly twelve hundred people and, Dear Heart, *in The Festival!*

As luck would have it, I'd heard that Siobhán was friends with Walter Matthau, whose voice, unlike Cary Grant's, was one I was able to do and so, to their chagrin, I got my own back, using Matthau's voice on my next couple of lines: 'Go to bed will you? And for God's sake get out of those clothes!'

I will never forget the expressions on the two upturned faces under the wide-brimmed hats: mock horror on the *grande dame*'s, a wide-eyed and mischievous 'you-naughty-boy!' look on the mug of the queen of comedy!

Over an après-show drink we declared it a draw.

May they both rest in peace.

JIM BARTLEY

If I was asked to describe Maureen in two words, they would have to be 'Maureen Potter', but having worked with Maureen for nearly a quarter of my working life, I wouldn't leave it at that.

In every profession, trade or business, you come across somebody you learn from. That somebody for me was Maureen. She was the very epitome of the term 'professional'; her temperament, attitude and concern for others were unique.

As she paced up and down in the green room before a show, she would ask how you were feeling, straighten your tie or with some other gesture reassure you and make you feel relaxed and comfortable.

She paid great attention to detail, not only to her own performance but also to all aspects of the show. While never interfering or intrusive, she did have a very definite opinion as to what would work or wouldn't work. She was always right!

She had great time for everybody in the show and always showed great concern for anyone who had been ill or had other problems; in a cast of over seventy performers, she knew every name. At times it seemed as if she knew the names of everyone in the audience too!

I always felt that, having had a couple of months' break after a strenuous season of Panto, she was most relaxed during the first week of rehearsals for *Gaels of Laughter*. She would arrive into the Tea Lounge of the Gaiety full of energy and great delight at meeting us all again. (She also loved adjourning to Neary's pub at lunchtime for a bit of 'catching up' and maybe a few suggestions for rewrites of certain sketches. Indeed, some scriptwriters used to dread the afternoon rehearsals, wondering if their sketches would survive the surgery. If they did, it has to be said, they were all the better for it.)

I have many memories of working with Maureen Potter, feel privileged to have done so – and to have been able to share a glass of 'milk' with her in the green room after the show.

BRENDAN GRACE

I heard about Maureen Potter long before I ever set eyes on her. I was always, indeed I am still, an avid listener of RTÉ Radio One (and I do remember when it was Radio Éireann!)

Maureen Potter and the character of her son Christy were featured on a radio programme, perhaps on Sundays. I had my own image of what Christy might have looked like. He was always in trouble. He had no voice and so was therefore just a figment of our imagination, but was totally real. That's how good she was. Her great ability was to paint a comic situation right onto the blackboard of your mind.

Then I saw her in Panto. Can't remember the year or the name of the Panto – didn't matter anyway; it was Maureen Potter and that was funny enough.

I first met her backstage at the wonderful Gaiety Theatre after a matinée performance in 1980. She was such a bubbly and welcoming person to me and my family; and later, in the mid-eighties, I had the great joy (and, indeed, the honour) of working on stage with her at the same theatre in *Robinson Crusoe*.

One of the sketches we performed together in that Panto was 'Sonny Boy', during which I would sit on her knee for the duration of the song. Night after night, it was by far the funniest highlight of the entire show and I can reveal at long last, I'm sure with Maureen's heavenly blessing, that her real knee was cleverly hidden by a wooden prop knee made by legendary stage manager George McFall.

So, despite how it looked on the night, I was not the reason she used a walking stick after that!

She was simply the best.

Maureen as Maisie Madigan in
Juno and the Paycock. Photo: Tom Lawlor

John Kavanagh

As a child, like most others I was taken to see Maureen Potter perform with Jimmy O'Dea at the Gaiety Theatre, Dublin, and never dreamed that one day I would share the stage with her. In Joe Dowling's acclaimed Gate Theatre production of *Juno and the Paycock,* we toured extensively with the show. We shared a camel (the four-legged sort) on the Mount of Olives when we performed the play in Jerusalem and a yellow taxi when we played on Broadway.

We again trod the boards together in Hugh Leonard's play *Moving* at the Abbey Theatre and I was honoured to be asked to take part in her tribute concert at the Gaiety Theatre.

She was an inspiration in more ways than one: performing nightly while suffering terribly with septic arthritis – pain that would have floored the toughest man, but not diminutive Maureen. It was a pleasure, an inspiration and a great, great honour to have known, worked with and loved a wonderful genius.

Geraldine Plunkett

'Oh darling, I'm as old as a field' – not a very funny line on paper, but coming from the inimitable Maureen Potter, it had the doctor in Manhattan wiping tears of laughter from his eyes.

It was 1988 and we were in his surgery because Maureen was getting treatment for the arthritis in her knees. She was in dreadful pain but, in spite of that, she had the doctor in stitches. As she was getting dressed, I told him she was Ireland's greatest comedienne. 'I am not a bit surprised,' he said, 'she is the funniest lady I have ever met.'

We were on Broadway doing *Juno and the Paycock* with the late Donal McCann and John Kavanagh and a wonderful cast in Joe Dowling's production for the Gate Theatre. The show was a great success and Maureen was a wonderful Maisie Madigan – hilariously funny and very touching in Act Three. No one in the audience, seeing her dancing around, could have guessed that she was in constant pain. Sometimes she could barely stand in the dressing room, but the moment she stood on stage she became totally alive; 'Doctor Theatre', as she said, always came to the rescue; but it wasn't just that – she had extraordinary courage. She never gave less than a hundred per cent and she simply loved performing.

Like many Dubliners, I can't remember a time when the names of Maureen Potter and Jimmy O'Dea weren't as familiar to me as those in my own family. Every Christmas, a very kind uncle used to buy us all tickets for the matinée of the Gaiety Pantomime on St Stephen's Day – it was the highlight of the year. We looked forward to it from early December (Christmas didn't start in September when I was a child) and relived every moment for weeks afterwards. Maureen, Jimmy, Danny Cummins and all the wonderful artistes who joined them year after year simply made Christmas for us.

Then, of course, there was *Gaels of Laughter* in the summer, and in her later years her show in Clontarf Castle where she again had the audience in the palm of her hand.

When I was cast in *Juno* with her, I was thrilled and honoured – and very nervous; the idea of sharing the stage with my childhood idol was overwhelming. But I needn't have been. She was warm, generous, helpful and it was an education to watch her develop her part, though she was very funny from the start. I shared a dressing room with her in the Gate and on tour in Edinburgh, Jerusalem, Broadway and again in the Olympia in 1990. She was thoroughly professional, with her place meticulously laid out: the exact amount of hair pins for her wig, her eye pencils and lipstick in a neat row and her costume carefully hung up in the correct order. She was always in the theatre for 6.30, even though Maisie Madigan did not appear until Act Two.

We had great chats and laughs about all sorts of things until about 7.30; then she would become quiet and start to get into the role. She never got over her nerves, which always amazed people. She said they got worse as she got older, though of course they never showed on stage.

She knew more about my costume than I did and kept a motherly eye on me. Once I put a waistcoat on inside out without noticing – she did though, and stopped me going on stage with '20th Century Props' written across my back!

Maureen enjoyed touring and was interested in everything. Through her I also had the great pleasure of getting to know Jack, her wonderfully supportive husband, her script writer and soul mate. He was her rock and came with her everywhere; a quietly funny man of great charm. He and her two sons were the centre of her life; she missed them dreadfully and rang Jack every day.

Unfortunately he could not come to New York so she and I spent a lot of time together. Because of the pain in her knees, we never went very far. There was a lovely little Greek restaurant near the hotel and we had lunch there most days. She got to know the waiters and, of course, made them laugh. They became terribly fond of her and made a special effort to get her whatever she wanted, as she did not eat much: a little liver and onion (very New York) and a little mashed potato followed by one scoop of ice-cream and a smidgen of chocolate sauce.

Since then, every time I taste ice-cream and chocolate sauce I think of Maureen – darling Mo Po – who gave more joy and pleasure than she ever realised to so many thousands, young and old alike. She was a comic genius, an extra-ordinary all-round performer – performer was a word she always used: not actor, singer, dancer or comic. It was a privilege, an honour and a joy to have worked with her.

Ní fheicimid a leithéid arís.

PART VI

Backstage

In small venues, work backstage is spread thickly on a handful of people, but when a show is in rehearsal or playing a run, a large theatre such as the Gaiety operates like a small, claustrophobic town populated by a single extended family, with all that this entails. And while the audience for the finished show sees the swan sailing along the lake, the silky presentation has been made possible, not only by the writer or playwright, but also by underwater toil. By a thousand hours of planning by producer, director and designers of sets, costumes, lighting and sound; by the hands-on work of music director, choreographer, fight expert, stunt co-ordinator, vocal and movement coaches, stage director, stage managers and their assistants, props men, electricans, lighting and sound technicians, stage hands, scene painters, carpenters, accountants; plus, in front of house, box-office, house manager, ushers, bar staff, sellers of programmes and interval ice-cream. By a personal dresser.

Whump! The star, dressed as The Widdy, in day-glo crinolines, aprons, mob-cap and comical boots, disappears off-stage.

Whump! She's back on in completely different gear, a sleek trouser suit in black velvet with shining white blouse and patent leather shoes. Hair combed nicely, glasses perched on the end of the nose.

'What's the record for the quick change for Maureen, Rosaleen?' Sadie Cuffe, former wardrobe mistress of the Gaiety, turns to Rosaleen Walsh, Mo's long-time dresser.

'Seventeen seconds,' she replies.

'And this'd be everything, shoes, tights, dress, everything!' Sadie is concerned that Rosaleen is being too modest. 'Rosaleen found a way to puddle the tights,' she explains, 'with the legs rolled into the feet so you could put them on in one go, didn't you Rosaleen, isn't that right?'

'That's right.' The dresser – who had the advantage of being the same size as her charge, so when she met Potter on the way off-stage for a quick change, she was shoulder to shoulder, head to head and hand to hand – remains modest.

Sadie herself substituted for Rosaleen one night when this tights feat had to be performed for Maureen, 'and I tell you, I was sweating. She was so particular.'

'Yeah, the *language* out of her!' This is Annie Cuffe, Sadie's ninety-year-old mother who, having preceded her daughter in wardrobe not only in the Gaiety but in every theatre and music hall in Dublin since 1913, is a repository of theatre lore. 'It was desperate. She'd F and blind ...'

US working-visa formalities are very restrictive where theatre is concerned and Rosaleen was not allowed travel to New York with Potter for *Juno and the Paycock*. As a result, there was nearly a disaster. 'She had this lovely black dress for Maisie Madigan, real period, with the lace all tatty.'

But the wardrobe person for the Broadway theatre took one look at this musty old piece of tat with which she was presented, ripped off the ancient, ragged lace, redolent with decades of stage lore – not to speak of stage muck – and replaced it all with nice stiff frills in nice new black net.

Sadie, Rosaleen and Annie are sitting together in the sunny tea-room of the Gresham Hotel on Dublin's O'Connell Street. They laugh like drains at the good of it. The tea-room is sparsely populated but at the next table they're laughing along. Not knowing quite why, because they're Italians.

When things again calm down, Rosaleen finishes the story, which, needless to remark, necessitated the said net frills being removed sharpish and the 'tat' being recovered from the wardrobe trash can to be replaced, stitch by painful stitch. 'And she said to me over and over: "Oh, I wish you'd been there with me!"'

To facilitate the quick changes, zips were taboo on Maureen Potter's Pantomime costumes. 'And you couldn't have even fasteners or anything like that. It had to be Velcro.' Velcro down the back and down the front too. Two rows of the stuff in case one would give. Plus, to be sure to be sure, rows of big poppers as well. So, as if she was opening two Ziplok bags, Rosaleen could unpeel the costume with two pulls.

These three women, who knew Maureen Potter as well as

or better than almost anyone else backstage at the Gaiety, confirm she had an exacting nature where work was concerned. In fact, they dreaded Maureen's costume parade, which never took place until all her outfits were complete and ready for the stage. 'She was a perfectionist and she wanted things done her way.' This is Sadie. 'She hated fittings, so they had all to be ready at the same time.'

To facilitate this, they set up a 'Maureen' dressmaker's dummy on which they based their cutting and draping so the star wouldn't have to submit to interim pinning and tucking. 'And when she came up to try on the costumes, she always brought Thelma with her.' This from Annie. 'Sitting there. Thelma was her pal and whatever Thelma said – but Thelma was all right. And Babs'd be gone. Hiding around the corner somewhere.' Babs Delmonte was the costume designer.

Maureen in her favourite black velvet suit.
Photo: James D. O'Callaghan

'Her favourite was always the black velvet trouser suit,' says Sadie. 'And the waistcoat with the white shirt and the big collar. Every single show. They were the ones I made for her – and if you know anything about velvet, you start out great and then at the end you're left with everything going the wrong way [she mimes opposing velvet piles between her fingers] but for her everything had to be perfect. We all loved Maureen, but she could be a walking divil. She was a Capricorn – like herself [she indicates her mother].'

'Yeah, she could be a walking divil.' Annie ignores the dig. 'We loved her but she made us really nervous. We loved her to bits but we were afraid of her. And it wasn't only the collar on the trouser suit: there had to be a huge white collar on every costume. I had to iron and starch every one of them to reflect the light on to her face.'

Defences and public masks are down backstage and these three were in a good position to observe the strengths and weaknesses of the clients they served. In particular, a star's long-term dresser is in a critical position to do so and, by common consent amongst the whole theatrical community, Rosaleen Walsh was not only Maureen's aide, but her confidante. Throughout this conversation in the Gresham, she contributes least and, in her own calm way, makes it clear she will never divulge anything she learned or heard during the course of her duties. She does make her quiet presence felt, however, usually with smiles of reminiscent agreement with the opinions of the other two, while never volunteering her own. Maureen Potter chose wisely here.

'Tell about the eleventh costume,' Sadie now prompts her mother.

Apparently, each Pantomime demanded ten complete changes of costume for its star. But no matter what happened to the original ten, they could be repaired but not replaced. 'Whatever she wore on the opening night, she had to wear the same ten all the way through the run. You daren't change them.'

So they darned and patched anything that got torn and checked the poppers and Velcro were in proper working order and that the increasingly fragile black velvet would hold up to its rough handling until the end of the run. They repaired the handmade little shoes: 'She was size two and a half – I'd make them for her.' Sadie takes up the running. 'She had them in all different fabrics, one for every different costume. And when they were made up, we'd get soles put on them. She loved those little shoes, didn't she Rosaleen?'

Rosaleen confirms that Maureen did indeed love her little shoes.

As for the eleventh costume, they always made it, despite the fact that it was completely redundant. 'I made eleven,' says Annie, 'because Babs, out of the goodness of her heart, would design another one. But after it was finished, Rosaleen would come in and say "She's not going to wear it."'

Rosaleen smiles an enigmatic confirmation of this.

'If she didn't wear it in the dress rehearsal,' Annie carries on, 'and she never did, that was it, she didn't wear it. But it had to be finished, and hung, in the dressing room. The rail had to be full. Even if you did that same show again she wouldn't wear that costume but still it had to be on the rail in the dressing room.'

'I remember walking the city one time' Once more, Sadie takes up the story. 'She wanted another costume for Aladdin because she was playing Aladdin and Babs wanted a certain turquoise blue. An elaborate fabric she wanted, she got that into her head. I walked the city, because there wasn't a great selection here. Anyway, I got it, laid it out, cut it, made it up on her block, finished it, brought it down to her and she just said to me, "Hang it there."' She points to an imaginary rail in an imaginary dressing room but so vivid is the picture in her own mind that it transmits instantly, complete with heat, smell of buckram, heavy cotton and stiffened taffeta from the hanging row of costumes, garish in the extra-bright light from bulbs around the make-up mirror. But that eleventh costume, like all the other eleventh costumes, never saw the footlights.

The first two weeks of a Pantomime played twelve shows a week – a matinée every day as well as the night show – so there was no time to wash or clean costumes. So they did their utmost to preserve the fabrics, issuing the cast with underarm dress shields and, because of all the quick changes, and ripping on and off, backing each of Maureen's with cotton lining. They also shrank all the materials in advance before each costume was constructed.

Maureen was not only queen of her stage, she was also queen of her dressing room. She had 'an old cloth, the same old cloth' on her table and used a regular toolbox to store her make-up. 'And any of the new cleaners came in,' says Sadie, 'I would have to send them a note and say "DO NOT TOUCH ANYTHING ON HER DRESSING TABLE." She'd do it herself. "And if you see something lying around somewhere," I'd tell them, "hoover around it but don't touch it."'

They riff on some of their more famous creations, like the ones they made for the wordless 'ballroom dancing' sketch featuring Potter and Danny Cummins, where he was the woman and she the man. When 'she' twirled full circle, 'he' would fly off, hooked to 'her' down along his front to the ecstatic hilarity of the audience. 'Huge big hooks, we had to use, a big double row. You'd want to see the *size* of them.'

And then there were the tutus. 'Real tutus too, they were,' says Annie. Pink net. Made for Eugene Lambert, Cecil Nash and Hal Roach ('Aa-hh, Hal!' They exchange loving glances. They all love and admire Hal.)

They don't like to be disloyal to anyone they worked with but they will say that while the same Danny was a brilliant comedian, he 'broke Maureen's heart' with his indiscipline. She hated ad libbing, 'with her it was script, script, script,' but he couldn't be prevented from wandering off it.

And there are some artistes they despise completely. No names, no pack drill, right? But the stories, although utterly libellous, are very funny.

Where Maureen's life outside the theatre was concerned, they cannot emphasise enough how important her sons were to her – 'She talked about them *all* the time'; and while others might profess wonder at the outward mismatch of the relationship between the bouncy, chatty star and her much quieter husband, they have a theory that all you had to do to understand it was to look at and listen to the scripts he wrote for her. 'It all came out in his writing for her,' says Sadie. 'You'd never know to look at or to talk to him that he'd have written those scripts.' They perform a quick, three-way visual Round Robin and, when it's clear they are all in agreement, Sadie continues as spokesperson: 'Through "Christy" and everything else, he said everything he wanted to say. He was her rock. He's just a very quiet man.'

Some of their most telling insights could be formed between matinée and night performance, where the tradition of 'The Wardrobe Tea' grew and prospered. They would clear the cutting table, 'And Mammy'd make a cake, wouldn't you, Mammy?'

Mammy nods. 'And we'd have a drink. She introduced us to brandy [Annie's drink of choice is still straight brandy, glowing amber on the table in front of her] and she loved her Philadelphia,' Sadie adds fondly. 'Do you remember her and her Philadelphia, Rosaleen?'

Rosaleen's turn to nod.

'She did that ad,' Sadie cuts in, 'butter is the cream – she loved butter and the Philadelphia, that was always her contribution to the tea. We'd all bring in something.'

'Maureen Toal' – Annie's turn again – 'she'd bring in the coddle,' and all three fall over themselves with reassurances that coddle – a Dublin dish of tripe, onions and pork sausages boiled in milk – was a great addition to Wardrobe Tea between the matinée and the evening performance.

So at Wardrobe Tea, Maureen, little legs swinging, would sit drinking her tea and her brandy and spreading her Philadelphia and eating her cake – while entertaining them all with 'funnier stories than you'd ever hear in the show'. Jokes. Stories about Fairview and her childhood, her sons, scurrilous stories about fellow thespians. Kind ones, too, about one of her real favourites, Cecil Sheridan: about the time he wandered in to Clerys in O'Connell Street to buy a tie, but when he got home he realised that he had left his little bag with all his pucks and pieces in it somewhere in the store. So he went back in to town but couldn't get into Clerys through the crowds because there was a bomb scare and they were just blowing up his bag. (She *loved* that one.) Or the time Sheridan stood in the rain for what seemed like hours to sign the book of condolences beside Louis Elliman's coffin but when he got up to it realised that the Jewish custom was to put money in. 'He hadn't a penny, so quick as a flash he stuttered: "J-j-just s-s-stepped in to s-s-see if everything was o-o-o-k!"'

'You'd be sick with the laughing. Do you remember the stuff about the Siamese cat?' Sadie asks the other two, who crack up. 'She had me in stitches about that flippin' Siamese cat,' goes Annie, 'and Fred came up once.' Her lips draw themselves into a thin straight line. 'Once.' She has suddenly remembered her claim that producer Fred O'Donovan still owes her money.

'Don't mind her,' Sadie warns. 'They get on great really.'

But Annie won't be deterred. 'He blamed it on Maureen. That Maureen had to get a percentage of the show and she wasn't getting enough. And then he said he had to get a new curtain for the stage and it cost six hundred pounds –'

The complaints are clearly ritual and well-worn because the others pooh-pooh them and get her to admit that, behind it all, Fred has a real kind heart. That he kept many a one going by making a part in the Panto for them when no one else would hire them because of the drink. (She names names. They all name names, plenty of them.)

The bottom line for these three women where Maureen Potter is concerned is that she represented everything that was good and exciting about their lives in theatre. 'People try to copy her but there'll never be another Maureen,' says Sadie to more great, nodding agreement. And while they had not worked with her for years because of her ill health, they do miss her terribly.

In fact, they pine terribly for theatre in general because

the business has changed completely. Costuming is generally now outsourced and their skills and experience, built over generations, are no longer required. It seems that while Maureen was the mammy of the backstage family, everyone was secure. As soon as she fell into bad health, her family did too.

The star herself was apparently aware of her unique status in Irish theatre, but with the gratitude for it went the dreadful responsibility. 'I'm always afraid I'll let them down.'

She worked her legs and hips, face and voice to virtual extinction in the service of that responsibility. As lately as 1999, when John Costigan, now in charge of her beloved Gaiety, was looking for funds to refurbish the frontage of the theatre, he asked her to accompany him when he went to seek funds from Séamus Brennan, minister in charge of the Millennium Committee. Although frail and in desperate pain at that stage, she instantly agreed. That they did get the money, he says, was due largely to her presence. 'I don't think we would have got it without her.'

'Long ago in the Gaiety,' says George McFall, the retired stage director of the Gaiety, 'we had charity shows practically every Sunday night. You see, those days the ordinary people had nothing and there was the Herald Boot Fund and the Lord Mayor's Coal Fund. And everyone worked for nothing. Their one day off, they'd come in and work. They still do it. They haven't changed.'

Maureen Potter was to the forefront of this charity effort, and *never* said 'no'.

Ireland being Ireland, however, you wouldn't want to get above yourself no matter who you are. For instance, once Potter and 'some of the gang' performed in a charity gig in Jury's Hotel, in the presence of the then President of Ireland, Eamonn de Valera.

When he was going he made a special point of coming over to her to say goodbye.

'Goodbye now, Betty,' he said.

Maureen checking re-furbishment plans for the Gaiety.
© RTÉ Stills Library

JOHN O'CONOR

My special connection with Maureen Potter came each time I would play as soloist with the RTÉ Symphony Orchestra in a subscription concert at the Gaiety Theatre, a regular venue before the National Concert Hall opened in 1981.

Sometimes, the concert would be on a Sunday night during the run of the Panto (they had Sundays off) and, as soloist, I was given the Number One dressing room – the room Maureen used during the week. I would walk into this tiny cubby-hole of a room with her make-up and costumes all around and have a secret communion with her. What helped most was the little note she always left, apologising for the state of the place and wishing me every success with the concert. I felt these notes were my good-luck charms and treasured every one.

My first memory of Maureen would have been in the fifties at the Gaiety Panto, an annual fixture in our house. I absolutely loved it and it was one of the highlights of the Christmas season.

The star, of course, was Jimmy O'Dea and he was loved by us all. Danny Cummins was also great gas and I used to delight in trying to emulate the mimes of Milo O'Shea (especially the one where he's an incompetent doctor doing an operation and forgets to put the heart back in at the end when he has already sewn up the patient!)

But for me the real star was Maureen. There was a pixie-like charisma to her on stage that meant that, even when Jimmy O'Dea was entertaining the audience, it was Maureen I watched. She seemed to get as much enjoyment out of Jimmy's jokes and antics as the rest of us and, indeed, it was because of her reactions that I enjoyed everything so much. When she shrieked with laughter, I shrieked with laughter; when she thought something was a bit naughty, so did I; when she asked us to warn the beautiful damsel that the baddie was about to pounce, I would be on my feet screaming a warning at the top of my voice. I trusted her totally and was absolutely spellbound by her.

I don't remember her having a solo in the first Pantos I saw but later on her solos were anticipated with feverish expectation. Most beloved of all were the Irish dancing skits – often with the unfortunate and invisible Christy in tow. Having done Irish dancing as a kid, I remember those *feiseanna* and she caught the atmosphere perfectly. No adjudicator ever got the result right, every other child was trying to do Christy down and those priggish little girls with the blond curls would have goaded anybody into attacking the curls with a scissors.

She could also do an imitation of a nun that would bring the house down. (I'm sure even the nuns would have been in fits looking at her.)

I never enjoyed the *Gaels of Laughter* quite as much because there were too many moments when Maureen wasn't on stage. I just didn't enjoy any of the other acts because they were periods to be endured while waiting for Maureen to reappear.

But I did love her as Miss Brannigan in *Annie* – although I knew she was only acting: our Maureen could never be that bad!

As for Joe Dowling, he was a hero for tempting her into 'straight' theatre and I'm sure Seán O'Casey would have become one of her greatest fans if he had ever seen her in one of his plays. I was so proud of the success she had later in life because of the opportunities Joe gave her.

She was so much a part of my life when I was growing up that I was proud to be with her on her last TV appearance. The bones may have creaked but her infectious smile never faded.

Even now I'm smiling as I think of her and those precious little notes she left me in 'our' dressing room at the Gaiety.

LIZ O'DONNELL

Speaking as a 'Dub', Maureen Potter, Jimmy O'Dea and Danny Cummins were huge personalities in my childhood.

I actually shared the Gaiety stage with Maureen Potter:

my sister Yvonne and I were part of a child dance group, The Oultons, and in the sixties we performed in Pantomimes both in the Gaiety and Olympia theatres. As a result, I have clear childhood memories of the smell of make-up, of the perfumed Gaiety Girls (the Gaiety's version of The Royalettes, who were the hoofers at the old Theatre Royal), of backstage pandemonium, of flaps in the dressing room and, of course, of the rousing finales featuring 'There's No Business Like Show Business'.

Maureen Potter was a unique performer, a quintessential Dubliner with a sharp wit and a warm heart; she was always kind to us child dancers and I never heard her raise her voice except as a character in performance. Children warmed to her especially, because she was our size and clowned about in a childlike way.

My mother, Carmel, has a unique laugh and I will always associate her laugh with the antics of Maureen Potter in the Gaiety Panto at Christmas.

⌒

You will have noticed many references to 'the green room'. By now it is probably obvious what this is – a space reserved for the actors before, during and after a show where they can rest, recuperate, celebrate success or mourn failure away from the voyeuristic eyes of outsiders. It is a privilege to be invited to join them there.

But why is it green?

The simplest and most logical explanation seems to be that green is the most restful colour – hospital wards, schoolrooms and psychiatric institutions favour it – and that actors need to cool down after the glare and dazzle of stage lights. And yet in the seventeenth century, where the term seems to have originated, the players performed on stages illuminated by candles or oil lamps.

There are other explanations, of course.

According to Tomás Mac Anna, the name arose because in the days when actors performed in the open air they used a shaded area or bower to change their costumes. This was known as the greening area – hence green room. Martin Fahy, former general manager of the Abbey Theatre, likes the version which is supposed to have originated in the USA. The actors' waiting-room was also the room where they were paid. As the dollar was green, this room got the colour too.

Hal Roach, on the other hand, believes it is a relict of old-style London actors who spoke to one another in rhyming slang. 'The stage was "the greengage" and when the two syllables were separated, as in "see you on (or in) the green, mate" the abbreviation became known as the actors' meeting place.

The term has even spread to television stations and, whatever its origin, no theatre of standing lacks a green room, or at least a little space reserved for the performers and called as such by them.

GERRY LUNDBERG

Maureen Potter was always part of our lives through the Gaiety shows, radio and later television, and anyone who's ever worked with her has special memories, not least of the anecdotes she could tell like no one else. I worked with her in the Gaiety many years ago and to this day some of those stay with me.

She was very encouraging to the young children in the show and always allowed two of the Billie Barrys (in turn) to stay at the side of the stage and watch their peers in action, as she felt that this way they could learn a lot about the 'business'.

Her dressing room was the Number One and outside it there was a small bench where a few of the children would wait for their call to the stage. Like children everywhere, once a door was closed they thought they couldn't be heard and one night she overheard two of them in conversation outside thus:

'Have you school tomorrow?'

'Yeah.'

'Wha' have yiz got?'

'English. Wha' have you?'

'Ele-KEW-tion! I HAY-RITT!'

Another story that gave her – and us – great laughs was about the ladies of at least sixty years of age who came backstage to congratulate her after the show. This, mind, would have been thirty or forty years ago. 'Maureen, a great show,' one of them said in all seriousness. 'I always come to see you in the Gaiety. Ma brought me to see you from the time I was six years old.'

If my maths are correct, that would have made Maureen about 133 when she died. (Although maybe not too unbeliev-able, as she 'gave' to the business more than anyone I can recall.)

When rehearsals for Panto took place in early December we would all be delighted, as the theatre would be heated from early on; the DGOS (Dublin Grand Opera Society) were on stage at night and the heat had to be on early in the day for the Opera Divas.

And there was fierce excitement one year when it was announced that a Hollywood film company would be using the Gaiety for a scene in the movie *Darling Lili*, starring Julie Andrews. Maureen was in heaven because her (modest) Number One had to have a separate shower installed and also more costume space. She could not wait to get back into the 'new' dressing room with all mod cons. It wasn't to last; she claimed that the shower broke after only a week and wasn't repaired for years.

True or not, it proves that our biggest star got on and did the 'gig' with no stupid demands.

Playing in the Panto chorus, I was aware that Anna, who looked after us all in the Gaiety green room, always made a fuss of having Maureen's sandwich ready at the end of each evening show. In my innocence, I assumed that Maureen always ate her sandwich in her dressing room and then joined us in the green room for her glass of milk.

We would all be drinking but Maureen would still be on milk and in surprisingly great form.

But when one night we got to stay very late, relaxing in the green room, laughing and talking, I couldn't help noticing that Maureen's milk was getting greyer and greyer as the night went on.

Innocent or wha'?

This was her 'sandwich', in reality whiskey-and-milk.

She was never demanding, and when she was it was always for the good of the show and not personal.

And yes, she was a brilliant actor and entertainer – but more importantly, she was funny, sincere and giving. A truly nice 'star'.

KEVIN HOUGH

One of the abiding regrets of my life now is that I didn't get to sing at Maureen Potter's eightieth birthday party. This was something we arranged and wisecracked about together as, early in 2004, I walked her back to her taxi from the National Concert Hall, where she had adjudicated a talent competition for me.

Maureen was a marvellous adjudicator, tough but fair and generous, as I discovered during an earlier outing we took when I was presenting a senior citizens' talent contest in May 2003 at the Abbey Theatre.

Although we never worked on stage together, I never missed a Gaiety Pantomime or a *Gaels of Laughter* and got to know her very well while producing a series of eight radio programmes (*Maureen Potter Looks Back*) in 1997, working with her and with her husband, Jack. The woman was wonderfully talented, as everyone knows, but in show business that's not enough; Maureen Potter was the professional's professional: tireless, always fully prepared and energised, always 'up for it'.

We became good friends during the series and, after finishing the recordings, continued to keep in touch.

I was so sad when she passed away just a few weeks after her last television appearance on the *Late Late Show*, when, as usual, she wowed her audience.

I will always remember her generosity, her incredible talent and the buzz of just being in her presence.

Dearest Maureen, may God always keep you in the palm of his hand.

JULIAN ERSKINE

I first met Maureen when I was eight years old. My father had arranged for me to watch a matinée of the Panto from backstage.

This was my first time to pass behind the curtain and enter the magical world of 'backstage'. I was brought to the star's dressing room, where she shook my hand and made such a fuss of me that I guessed I had to be the most important visitor she had had all week, possibly all year. I was then brought to the side of the stage, where I climbed up a steel ladder onto a platform that housed the lighting board.

Lighting board is a modern term: in those days it was a Heath Robinson piece of machinery consisting of rows and rows of wheels and levers and it was operated by two men, who throughout the show spun wheels, tightened and loosened levers as they rode up and down on the wheels and all this in semi-darkness. For a small boy it was pure magic, like being invited onto the footplate of a steam engine and being taken for a trip.

But out on the stage the real magic was happening. I watched the show through the gap in the masking curtains, and it was an extraordinary afternoon, watching Maureen Potter in full flight, singing, dancing, tumbling, tripping, laughing.

I also had the double pleasure of seeing her operating off-stage too, dashing backwards and forwards to her dressing room for quick changes, joking with both cast and crew off-stage then bounding back on stage again.

And once, on her way on stage, she looked up at me and winked. I'll never forget that. In the midst of all that was going on, she remembered that there was a boy on the lighting platform who had come in to see her.

At the curtain call then came the ultimate small-heartbursting-with-pride moment. In the long, long list of names that she never failed to memorise, she mentioned mine!

Afterwards she asked me all about the show and gave me the time to answer her. Generous to a fault.

Years later I was the stage director for the newly formed Irish Theatre Company and we were rehearsing in the Gaiety one February. Ray McAnally was the show's director and one afternoon, while rehearsing on stage, I noticed a small figure creeping across the back of the stage, desperate not to interrupt, but Ray had spotted her and he stopped rehearsals.

He stood up and addressed the cast: 'I would draw your attention to the time. It is now 4.30. Tonight's Panto does not begin until 8 p.m. It has been running for two months. Maureen Potter has just come in to prepare for the show. I need say no more; that, ladies and gentlemen, is a consummate professional.'

He was right; there is no need to say any more.

If theatre people argue about the origins of the term 'green room', they are equally divided about the origins of some of the superstitions to which they almost universally subscribe.

Take the 'Scottish Play'. (It is difficult to name it even here in a book, in case of hex. Let's just call it 'Shakespeare's M-bth'.) If naming it is bad, quoting from it – horrors! – is even worse. And if the taboo is inadvertently breached, the only remedy is to leave the room or stage instantly, go somewhere else and, while rotating on one's own axle, recite three times, 'Fair thoughts and happy hours attend thee/fair thoughts and happy hours attend thee/fair thoughts and happy hours attend thee,' from Shakespeare's other great play, Hamlet. *Theatre people recount gory stories of people dying while working on this play, of people breaking limbs, people losing loved ones.*

George McFall is a fount of wisdom in this area and, because of his long service to theatre, his versions of the origins do make sense.

For instance, with regard to the Scottish Play, he says that in the old days it was very popular with audiences. 'So if you were in any other play and it wasn't doing business, the management would say, "We'll take it off and do the Scottish play," putting you out of work. You dreaded hearing that. So it got the reputation of being unlucky.'

Whistling in the vicinity of a theatre is another widely abhorred practice but he has a commonsense explanation for that one too. In the old days, he says, there was no way of communicating between the flies and the stage. ('The flies' is a cavernous space high above the stage; it is laced with heavy ropes, pulleys, wires and rows of hanging stage cloths – painted canvas scenery, ready to be 'flown' in.) Most of the fly men were sailors who came in on ships. They'd be in port for five or six weeks while the ship was being turned around for her next voyage and, being skilled on riggings, took temporary jobs in the fly towers of the local theatres. 'So the only way the stage manager could signal them to take a cloth out or drop one in was by using a little whistle. That's how the superstition grew …'

Because if you were crossing anywhere beneath the fly tower when the whistle blew, you'd be in danger of being felled by a few hundredweight of cloth.

MYLES MCWEENEY

Years ago, when my step-daughter, Ciara, was about nine years of age, we took her and a few of her friends to the Gaiety Christmas Pantomime starring Maureen Potter. The show, as always, was great and there was much cheering and clapping from the audience throughout.

But to the acute embarrassment of her mother and me, Ciara had recently perfected, after much headache-inducing practise, a strange shrill whistle, which, in lieu of conventional applause, she now used (frequently) to register her approval of the show.

Her warble earned her some raised eyebrows in the theatre, but, thankfully, she soon bored of it.

After the show, as a treat because it was a special day for Ciara, Maureen had invited us back to her dressing room for a chat. The other kids were awed by being in the presence of Maureen Potter, clad in a silk dressing-gown but with her full stage make-up still in place. Ciara, however, something of a backstage veteran, immediately asked the star of the show if she'd heard her whistle, demonstrating her newly acquired and highly anti-social skill.

'Oh, my goodness,' Maureen exclaimed, recoiling from the sharp blast a few inches from her face: 'so you were the person whistling in the auditorium!

'Didn't you know that *nobody* whistles inside a theatre? It brings very bad luck. Bad luck that lasts for years and years.' (She said this quite seriously, and I still don't know if whistling really is as much of a theatrical no-no as wishing an actor good luck or mentioning the name of 'that' play.)

Ciara looked suitably crestfallen with this news, but brightened considerably when Maureen added: 'But there is something you can do to lift the curse. It's a special spell. You have to go outside, turn round three times, knock on the door and when I say, "Come in", you come back in, close the door quietly and swear.'

Delighted, Ciara ran to the door, banging it shut behind her, did three quick spins outside and was back in a trice, standing in front of Maureen, riveted, with her mouth working but no sound emerging.

'You have to swear, dear,' Maureen said helpfully. 'Say dash it, or blast it or darn it ...'

'**** it!' exploded Ciara. '**** it! **** it! **** it!'

'Oh, dear me,' said a startled Maureen, eyes like saucers, 'my husband says that sometimes, but only when something terrible has happened like when he bangs his thumb with a hammer, and he usually only says it once.'

'Oh, my Mummy says it all the time,' said Ciara.

Maxi – Irene McCoubrey – is the popular presenter of RTÉ'S early morning music show Risin' Time. *Dick – Barbara Lawlor, née Dixon – is now vice-president of a real estate company in Canada. (She says she later regretted that choice of name but was given it when she was only twelve years old and didn't 'get' it!) Twink (Adèle King) is the multi-talented performer who followed Maureen Potter as a headliner in Panto. She runs three theatre schools using the acronym AKTS (Adèle King Theatre Schools). Fred O'Donovan plucked these three from their school group, The Young Dublin Singers, to become the trio Maxi, Dick and Twink.*

IRENE McCOUBREY

I have a dear friend who once gave me a great piece of advice. 'Look very carefully at your watch,' he said. 'Is it going forward or backward?'

Not a lot of people welcome the passage of time and, in show business particularly, not a lot of established artists, looking critically in the mirror or fearfully over their shoulders, welcome the young. Even fewer take time out to give advice to the inexperienced.

Maureen Potter did both.

I met her in God's time, when Adèle King, Barbara Dixon and I (as Maxi, Dick and Twink) took part with her in Pantomimes and summer shows at Dublin's Gaiety Theatre.

To say she was talented, funny (on stage and off), professional and unselfish is only to re-state what is universally known about her but I was lucky enough to experience it first hand.

So what did she teach us?

Where do I start?

She taught us to be punctual, to respect our fellow artists, to prepare for performances, never to miss the half-hour call, to listen every day to the news of the day so our patter and script would be right up to date and – importantly – to leave our own troubles at the stage door. Our job was not to share our woes, but to help those people out there in the seats to forget theirs.

She taught us also how to pace, both ourselves (not to burn the candle at both ends) and the act we gave on stage. She taught us to prepare for each ad lib; to listen carefully to the audience each night so as to become aware of reactions and, therefore, changes that could still be made to scripts and performances in order to make each show that one shade better and fresher each time.

She taught us to respect the team of people it takes to put a show together and to look the audience collectively and individually in the eye, be it in the theatre or on television or with only the medium of voice on radio.

And she taught us that when the show was over, and everything possible had been done, there was always time to meet an old friend or make a new one.

Maureen, you are much loved and never forgotten and if there hasn't been a variety show in heaven to date, there is now.

Barbara Lawlor

Maureen Potter was 'The Star' and I was a singer in the chorus. I was ten and in awe.

The word 'trooper' belonged, still belongs, to her and she set the bar high for us kids. I remember when she lost her voice due to laryngitis but went on anyway and, through her hoarseness, reached out to that audience with the energy and magic that came from her soul. They responded to her and they loved her even more.

She inspired me, all of us, and instilled a sense of professionalism that the three of us, Maxi, Dick and Twink, have continued to live by throughout our careers.

It was a thrill to pass her backstage or meet her in the green room going to and from our various entrances and exits from the stage – she always had a friendly word, a compliment or encouragement and even at such a young age

– ten through twelve – made me feel like I belonged. That I was valuable.

One of her popular lines at the time was 'God never closed one door but He opened a row of cottages.'

Well, Maureen, to quote Sweet Charity, *If they could see me now, that little gang of mine* ...

I live in Canada now, where I'm Senior Vice-President of Baker Real Estate Corporation and a Fellow of The Real Estate Institute of Canada. I consult with architects, developers, construction workers and interior designers – and then, when the building is finished, I sell it!

I can see your mouth in that big round 'O'! I can see your eyebrows reaching for your scalp! I can hear your voice: 'There's posh!'

Far from the Gaiety stage, eh? But with Maxi's broadcasting career, my condominiums and Twinkle's theatre schools, your cottages have flourished, Maureen, not least due to that early training in work ethic and in striving for excellence. Thank you. You will not be forgotten.

ADÈLE KING

There is a small little corner backstage in the Gaiety Theatre, at the downstage left entrance, which, for most of my childhood there, my darling old stage manager, George McFall, called 'Adèle's corner'.

On mature reflection, it should have been called 'Adèle's learning corner', for it was from that little corner that I spent so many hours, day and night, year in year out, watching the Grand Master, Maureen Potter, at work.

Procuring a place in the wings during any hectic big production is no mean feat, particularly when I had a number of major obstacles to overcome.

First, the productions then were gargantuan ... Fred O'Donovan once proudly advertised a show that boasted a cast of seventy-six people!

Second, I was a very small child and they liked us to be in

either of two places at all times: on stage or, even better, in our dressing rooms.

And third, for most of those years, the backstage 'he who must be obeyed' was none other than the rather formidable figure of one Jimmy Potter ('Mr Potter' to us), stage manager of all Eamonn Andrews Studio productions there – and brother of the great lady herself, Maureen Potter ('Ms Potter' to us!)

Looking back now, George reckons that it was a combination of begging Jimmy Potter enough times to drive him mental, and showing a genuine interest in watching and learning, that afforded me that much-coveted place in the wings.

Whatever the reason, I now realise that I probably owe most of my theatre and performing career to date to the privilege of having my own private little master classes all those years, from one of the great performers of our time.

There wasn't a dance step of hers – from 'The Irish dancer with the apron full of medals' to the hysterical ballroom dance duets with Danny Cummins – that I couldn't do. There wasn't a duet with Milo O'Shea or Patricia Cahill that I couldn't sing. There wasn't a sketch from 'Christy at the Feis' to 'Ada and Maudie' that I didn't know word for word. There wasn't a rapid-fire costume change that I hadn't worked out the 'hows, whys and wheres' of.

I never fully understood as a child why I was so drawn to spend so many hours in the same spot:

Watching, listening and learning!

Watching, listening and learning!

It really wasn't until I became a headline act in the Gaiety myself that all the pieces started to fit.

I will never forget the opening night of *Babes in the Wood* in Christmas 1989. I had just given birth to my first baby, Chloë, in June of that year, so bouncing out of Holles St with a new baby, and bouncing into the gym for a new body, made for a very exciting and busy year.

The opening night would probably have gone in a

complete haze of what we call the 'my God we made it!' bewilderment that most opening-night casts feel, were it not for a knock on my dressing room door from the afore-mentioned Mr McFall. He had called – with tears in his eyes – to congratulate 'the little girl from the corner' for making it all the way to being the new headliner.

It hit me like a brick.

I'd been so busy with the endless weeks of endless rehearsals (and a new baby) that the thought had never occurred to me.

I thanked him for all the love and support he'd shown me since those distant days.

When the backstage area had quietened down a little and most of the opening-night-party revellers had thronged to the green room for the usual 'sweetie-luvvy-dahling' stuff, I took myself over to 'that corner', and in the almost pitch black darkness of the unlit stage, with only the hauntingly eerie light that always seems to seep from some inexplicable source, I took myself back in time.

I remembered being 'that little girl' watching Mo Po's every move.

Then I thought of the character I had just played that very night, and I realised how many of the dance moves, the facial gestures, the comic timings I had employed now in my own adult career.

I realised just how much I had learnt from that wonderful woman.

It was with the greatest of pleasure that on the closing night of that very run Mo Po was the theatre guest in the dress box and I was able to pay that tribute to her, live, in front of twelve hundred people.

They gave her a standing ovation.

It was to my utter delight that I got to meet and work with her in the National Concert Hall, only a matter of weeks before her death.

This time, both of my daughters, Chloë and Naomi, got to meet her, and a couple of my AKTS pupils as well.

The kids were enchanted at the opportunity of meeting a legend who was as caring, articulate, sharp, witty and terrific as ever.

The night in question added to my long list of wonderful memories.

There was never anyone like her, and there never will be.

Thank you ... For absolutely everything, Maureen!

Maureen with Twink at the NCH. *Courtesy of Adèle King*

ANNE BUSHNELL

1925 was a very good year for the future of show business and the movies: Sammy Davis Junior and Alan Bergman (*The Windmills of My Mind* and *What Are You Doing the Rest of Your life* with Michel Legrand and *The Way We Were* with Marvin Hamlisch) were born in New York; and, on 3 January that year, Maureen Potter was born in Dublin.

The song 'Non Je Ne Regrette Rien', written in 1959 by Georges Moustaki for Edith Piaf – and which she said summed up her life – could also have been written for Mo. Another, 'Applause-Applause!' written by Burton Lane and Ira Gershwin – and introduced in *Give a Girl a Break* in 1953 by Debbie Reynolds and Gower Champion – could also have been written for her, because she left the stage, all of her life and throughout her long and marvellous career, to cheers and the sound of thunderous hand-clapping. And as we all know, to all performers, actors, singers, dancers, musicians, magicians, in fact anyone on a stage, there is no greater sound.

After a Maureen Potter show, an audience always left the theatre happy, smiling, mesmerised by her unique talent, energy and photographic memory. I remember as a little girl we went to stay in my granny's the night before the Panto. We couldn't sleep with excitement and then, next day, we went to Woolworths in Grafton Street for an ice-cream cornet or a tuppenny wafer. When you walked through the doors and saw the safety curtain, it was wonderland. You could feel the excitement. I didn't want it to end – and who can forget the long list of names and dates and dedications she memorised at the interval and read out at the end? Every time I was on stage with her, I was overwhelmed by this aspect of her talent, for she had a wonderful brain – bless her.

She also had the ability to have the audience rolling in the aisles with laughter, before she even opened her mouth.

She was, quite simply, a superstar.

In fact, she reminded me of so many incredible stars, all rolled into one: Lucille Ball, Debbie Reynolds (as a young singer/dancer, Maureen would have been wonderful in *Singing in the Rain*), Barbra Streisand (she turned down the offer of *Funny Girl* because her son was on the way).

Really, Maureen could have played anything: *Call Me Madam, Calamity Jane, Annie Get Your Gun* – the list is endless.

She was very well respected by her peers. When we were on stage with her, we knew we were in the presence of a genius. I, for one, learned so much from her – especially timing, which is so important on stage and is an art in itself.

In the green room after the shows, where we all relaxed and unwound with her, she was just as funny, with marvellous stories and incidents. She gave us a whole other show. It was magic. I remember, particularly, the three or four months myself and my friends Pat and Jean spent with her during the long run of the show *Annie* at the Gaiety. She was playing Miss Hannigan, who ran the orphanage, and she was stunning; I saw other productions of this show afterwards but no one ever matched her performance.

Maureen always called me 'Bush'. Like her, I had danced in all-Ireland dancing competitions and had a bib full of medals; like her, I also did spots in Cine Variety in the Queen's Theatre and the Theatre Royal.

On 22 February 2004, I was a guest at the Dockland's Junior Talent Contest at the National Concert Hall where she was one of the judges, with Twink, Brendan Balfe and Dublin's Lord Mayor, Royston Brady. As we hadn't seen one another for some time, we hugged and laughed and talked; and afterwards, we all sat around and had a marvellous, nostalgic chat, exchanging stories. Maureen was in great form; she even did an interview for a radio station.

Twink had her camera with her that night and took photos of Maureen and me; then she had some taken of herself with 'our' star and friend. I'm thrilled and honoured to have mine, since I believe that these photos have to be the last ones taken.

Maureen with Anne Bushnell. *Courtesy of Adèle King*

Tony Kenny with Maureen and Noel Pearson.
Courtesy of Tony Kenny

TONY KENNY

A persistent buzzing sound, irritating and very far off, was disturbing my sleep. *I'll ignore it*, I thought, *and it might stop*. But it didn't stop and, as I slowly came to, I realised it was coming from the phone and the easiest thing to do would be to answer it.

Who could be calling at this unearthly hour? It couldn't be more than ten o' clock ...

'Hello?' I croaked.

'How would you like to do *Gaels of Laughter* at the Gaiety next summer?' It was the voice of Noel Pearson, recently appointed as producer of *Gaels* by Eamonn Andrews Studios. Even in that half-awake condition I realised this would mean working with the great Maureen Potter; this was an opportunity I was not going to miss.

Although I had appeared with Maureen previously, in several charity concerts and in an RTÉ 'Christmas special' directed by John McColgan, the thought of being up close and personal during rehearsals while Maureen was putting the magic together was something I was really looking forward to.

Well, what an education it proved to be! The extent of her knowledge and stagecraft, coupled with her ability to deliver and her ever-helping hand, was an experience I will never forget.

Maureen's many talents and her ability to really touch an audience have been well documented and admired, but I would like to highlight another side of her, a side we don't often hear about, and that's her willingness to share her great knowledge and stagecraft with every other member of the cast, particularly the younger entertainers.

For instance, I remember that during rehearsals for that *Gaels* we were doing a sketch called 'Marrying Mary', in which Maureen was playing Mary's mother, Mrs Mulligan. I was supposed to be Mary's boyfriend but Mrs Mulligan wasn't keen on me as a suitor for her daughter. In her opinion, her daughter would be far better off with Cyril, a travelling sales- man played by Vernon Hayden ('I travel in ladies underwear.')

At one point I enter while Maureen as Mrs Mulligan is baking cakes for this Cyril. 'Hello, Mrs Mulligan. I see you're baking my favourite cakes!' and I pick one up.

'They're not for you!' She knocks the cake out of my hand.

Now that's a simple enough bit of stage business. But when we finished the sketch, Maureen came over to me and asked me to hang on after the rehearsal: 'I have an idea.'

What happened after that rehearsal was a master class in stagecraft. 'Tony,' she said, 'you know that business with the cake? I think we could get great fun out of that.' And the two of us spent the next hour going through it again and again, she giving me instructions until she was happy.

When we eventually got to do the piece on stage, I would tee up for Maureen by taking up the cake and she would then slap it out of my hand, hard, so it would fly right out into the audience. I would pick up another one and she would do the same – and so on, a dozen fairy cakes every show. She got so good at it she could actually take aim and hit specific people in the audience, always saving the last one for Thelma Ramsey, her musical director and great friend, who was in the orchestra pit in front of the stage. Poor Thelma got a fairy cake right between the eyes every night. By the end of the scene the whole audience would be in hysterics, but no one more so than Thelma, who had a most infectious laugh.

I'm glad to say Maureen and I became great friends, and I went on to do Pantomime with her, where again she never missed an opportunity to help.

I particularly remember with great fondness the nights in the green room where Maureen gave some of her finest performances. She could recall and perform pieces she had not done for years, for example from shows she had done during her days on the road in the fit-ups – touring performances, so-called because the players would hit a town and fit up the show themselves, sometimes for just one night. So there was that amazing memory again, well documented by those lucky enough to have their names called out by her at the end of each Panto without prompt, script or cue card.

When Maureen left the Gaiety and went to Clontarf Castle to perform in cabaret, she showed that she could adapt to this medium with the minimum of fuss. She enjoyed great success there too and proved (as if she needed to) that there is no substitute for real talent.

I was in America when Maureen died and heard of it through another phone call; I knew she had not been well but it still came as a shock – somehow she had seemed to be invincible. It was hard to grasp that no more would we be told, if we didn't like her show, to: *Keep your breath to cool your porridge!*

EMER O'KELLY

Mo would probably have liked me to 'keep my breath to cool my porridge'. But it's very difficult, just six weeks after her death, as I write this and look at some of the supposed obituary tributes paid to one of our very few incandescent stars. They reek of condescension, describing this unique dynamo as a 'popular entertainer' and mentioning in passing that, although her formal education ended at the age of twelve, she was 'highly intelligent'. On second thoughts, maybe Maureen Potter would have wanted me to blow up a storm: she had no time for pretension and snobbery, theatrical or otherwise.

Maureen on stage during the Gaiety tribute. Courtesy of Abhann

Potter was a star because every inch of her miniscule body housed an actor's soul: an actor observes the human condition and translates it to the stage. And that's what Mo did, spectacularly, accurately, lovingly and mischievously. She hadn't an easy life in her youth; her father died when she was only seven years old. Despite the fact that she was only persuaded into school with a promise of dancing classes to balance the torture, nobody, least of all her loving mother, would have wanted such a scrap of humanity to be a full-time working professional at the age of twelve. But that's what happened to Mo, and she never looked back from those early years performing in Britain with Jack Hylton, working with an altered birth certificate because she was too young to be legal.

When she recalled those pre-war years, she always told the funny stories, the heart-warming anecdotes; but a little girl must have seen and felt an awful lot of heartbreak beyond her years. One would like, perhaps, to say that, as she became one of our great luminaries in her middle age, life became a more serene business. But there was nothing serene about Mo: she continued to be restless, inventive, always looking for even greater perfection. She wasn't easy to work with: the more honest of her admirers in the profession will admit it. She was as tough as old boots, in fact, knowing that she was the one who carried the show and demanding the same standards from everyone else that she imposed on herself.

In my early years as a reporter, and working the Saturday-night diary shift, I would often drop in backstage at the Gaiety during the Pantomime or *Gaels of Laughter*. Mo was always ready to sacrifice her short break between sketches to give me a sparkling and original take on what was happening out front; and she would always grin wickedly and poke the reality line: 'Nothin' on tonight, love, I see.'

I used to tell her that people preferred her on the back page of their Sunday papers to a group photograph of four hundred dinner-jacketed accountants. 'Don't mock them, love,' she said. 'They're the ones who'll be laughing when we're both wondering what happened our pensions.'

She wasn't in it for the money; she was in it because, like all artists, she had to make her own particular art: she had to perform. And she didn't have understudies to cover the matinées: Mo worked herself to the point of self-flagellation, even when she had to keep herself going with doses of Scotch and milk because she was too sick to keep food down, probably through exhaustion.

She also had immense dignity and courage. When her performing career reached a premature end due to the crippling arthritis that blighted her later years with agonising pain, Mo didn't retire to the 'old actors' home' she used to make jokes about. She could have lived in happy retirement with her beloved Jack and spent time doting on her grand-children. But Maureen Potter may not have been able to appear on stage, yet she was still part of 'the profession'. She was always available to lend support to fellow actors, particularly when they had worked with her in the past. She and Jack were frequently seen at plays when she was barely able to stand with pain. She had surgery, but the pain went on. I watched her on one occasion in Andrews Lane Theatre, where there is no centre aisle. She and Jack were early in their seats, so had to get up and down to allow people past them. Every time she struggled to her feet her face was contorted with pain, the sweat on her forehead making her eyes sticky.

'Should you even be here?' I asked hesitantly.

'Wouldn't miss it, pet,' she said. 'I promised Rosie [Rosaleen Linehan, who was appearing on stage]. Anyway, isn't it only great to see yourself?'

But I think my favourite memory of her late years was a simple phrase that brought a packed ballroom to howls of laughter. It was the occasion of an eightieth-anniversary tribute to the late and much-loved Christopher Casson (he had first appeared on stage at the age of four, even more of a trooper, it could be said, than Mo herself). Four hundred people attended the celebration dinner organised by Michael Colgan in the Berkeley Court Hotel. Every theatrical luminary in the business said the few words, but it was Mo who shook the walls. She dragged herself to her full four feet eleven, composed her face solemnly, gathered pretty well every eye in the house, took a deep breath and enunciated 'Howaya, Chhrissstttyyy?' And for a lovely, loving moment, we were all back in the Gaiety Theatre.

The guest of honour had tears in his eyes; so had most other people. Maureen Potter was an enchantingly funny, kind and discerning woman in private life; as a comedy actor she was professionally tough, difficult and exacting: not a saint, just a star, the like of which has seldom been seen.

PART VII

An Enigma

So, as Phyllis Ryan asks, did we appreciate her enough during her lifetime? After all, this was a star stage performer who could act successfully in film and television, could carry a radio show, could dance, sing, headline a variety show, dominate the genre of Pantomime and could more than hold her own in 'legitimate' theatre with 'straight' artistes such as Siobhán McKenna, Donal McCann, Micheál MacLiammóir and Ray McAnally.

We did give her pieces of glassware and scrolls and an Honorary Doctorate from Trinity College and the Freedom of Dublin city, we did cheer her to the rafters one night when John McColgan produced that gala tribute show to her in her beloved Gaiety, but did we truly know the calibre of the woman who made herself available to us for such a long time for the price of a seat in the stalls? Her lifestyle began modestly and remained so. This was apparently her wish, because her family life with Jack and their two sons, Hugh and John, was paramount – but should we have done more to give her the official status she deserved? In other words, should she have been honoured and financially rewarded by the state?

Did we demand it?

And how good was she?

Hal Roach, by common consent amongst his peers one of the best, if not the best, stand-up comedian Ireland has ever produced, believes she was unique – but 'an enigma' too.

Hal Roach played for many years with Maureen Potter in *Gaels of Laughter*. Now working for much of the year abroad, particularly in the US, where he and his wife, Mary, maintain a home on an island close to Miami, Florida, he spends only three months a year in their beautiful house on eight acres, high above the village of Stepaside in the Dublin mountains. Just as in Fred O'Donovan's house, the view from every room is towards the sea but with this difference: Fred's house is on a cliff with the sea right below, filling the air – and the house – with its sound and smell. Hal's view is towards the sea too but the eye is drawn to it across the boroughs and villages of

Dublin, the cranes, the ships attending harbours, the pockets of housing tucked into folds of green landscapes to the south, the mountains to the north. He is justly proud of it.

He went to see Maureen Potter the week before she died. Sitting out on a chair beside her hospital bed, she was in good spirits, putting on a brave face and delighted to see him, but very frail, the once round face scrunched like a squirrel's – as evidenced by her appearance on that final *Late Late Show*, where she seemed to have shrunk even further into her already tiny frame.

Despite all the praise heaped on her by others – for her gutsiness, for the way she fired up under the lights, for her stentorian and word-perfect delivery of the ancient Cecil Sheridan parody – he believes (as do the three backstage women in the Gresham, Sadie and Annie Cuffe and her dresser, Rosaleen Walsh) that she should not have gone on that show; that although she shone, people talked about it afterwards in the context of her illness. 'I think we should have all been left to remember her the way she was on stage. That's certainly the way I would want to remember her.'

So why did she do it?

'Maureen Potter was an enigma – there's never been anything or anyone like her,' he says, before going on to explain about the universal craving of comics for the to-and-fro of live performance. For applause.

And indeed, there was a telling moment during that *Sunday Tribune* interview of the eighties at Clontarf Castle with Potter. Towards the end, a happy excited wedding party arrived; as they passed through to the function room, they glistened with good humour and the pleasure of such an occasion and the beautiful, sunny day. Quite soon, the sound of faint applause came from their room. It was obviously something to do with the wedding but, in her chair, Potter started and reflexively pivoted to meet it. (She caught herself at it and turned back with a rueful smile.)

Therefore, Hal Roach's explanation as to why a woman within weeks of her death would put herself through the nerve-racking ordeal of live television is more than plausible. She was driven, as he is, by the universal craving of comics for the feedback of audience.

His views dovetail with the inspiration behind films such as *The Entertainer*, novels, plays (*The Sunshine Boys*), scholarly psychological studies and also what most people splitting their sides in cabaret venues and theatres around the world secretly suspect: 'Comedians are psychotic, neurotic and schizophrenic. All of us.'

Including Maureen Potter?

'She more than any of us.'

He amends this a little: 'Well, of course Maureen wasn't strictly a stand-up. She was more a comic actress, but she did stand-up too.

'You see, comedians are born; you can teach the piano, trumpet or violin but you can't teach someone to be funny. It's inherent. Everything you do, leading up to the time when you suddenly realise you're a comedian, is just a stepping-stone to what you were born to do. And once you realise you're a comedian, your Calvary begins.'

A little dramatic, perhaps?

'I'm serious. I wouldn't wish a comedian's life on anybody. It's a lonely life.' Then, echoing what Billie Barry says of her friend ('Maureen lived from Panto to *Gaels* to Panto, always looking forward with very little in between'), he expands. 'The only time you live is when you're on. That's why comedians play golf every day. Anything not to think about reality. Until that *thing* happens at night and then –' his eyes light up as his hands embrace a Coliseum of attentive and appreciative side-splitters '– you're back! What happens is you're loved again. You live to see people laughing and in the adulation of it.'

He gives an example. 'Fifteen hundred people came to see me in Chicago. They stood up as one to applaud at the end. Well, you can't buy that. You *have* to get that again. You're walking on air and the whole body is satisfied, the mind too. You're on a high, it's like a drug, it's an addiction, it's the *highest* addiction.

'Then you go to the dressing room and you have a shower and you dress and you come back out and you pass it: this dark empty place that half an hour ago was magic.

'You *have* to do it again.

'But there's a whole day before it can happen, so what do you do? You can't play golf *every* day.' He shrugs. Then confesses that what he does is to clean his house.

Showbiz people, more than those in other professions, surround themselves with memorabilia of their shows, awards and functions in their honour. They fill their walls with photos of themselves with people they've met who might be more famous than they; their cupboards are stuffed with collections of their programmes, old newspaper cuttings and fan letters – all possibly to fill the void. Because during the 'off' times they need validation that the 'on' life really happened and can happen again.

'Comedians should never marry. You can ask her,' Roach gestures towards the kitchen where his wife is making coffee for us. 'You can't be married and be a showbiz comic. You can't share what you have with them. They're alone most of the time when they're with you on tour. For instance –' again he gives an example '– Mary was with our daughter in Vancouver and I flew her down to where I was and she did the rest of the tour with me.

'So she has a choice now. When I'm working, she can sit in the dressing room every night, knitting or reading a newspaper – or she can stay alone in the hotel. After each show, I sell tapes and records and my books so it's yet another hour before I get back to her. It's miserable for her.'

This view of the loneliness, not only of the spouse, but also of the comic him or herself, was endorsed years ago by several of Roach's peers in the course of research for a newspaper article about him for the *Sunday Tribune*.

'It's the loneliest and most difficult of all jobs in show business,' said one. 'You stand alone, with no props or set, nothing but your own wits.'

A solo singer can give a mediocre performance and still

garner polite applause, but on a bad night the stand-up encounters disembodied titters, heckling, booing and even missiles. There is no other member of a team on whom he can place blame. Roach himself has told friends that after such a night he has been known to go down to stand beside a dark river. At the very least, he will lie awake all night endlessly re-running the show in his head, re-living every flat gag, every leaden silence.

And for that *Tribune* article, in interview, he told the self-deprecating story of a performance in a workingmen's club in the north of England where he had been pelted with beer mats. He was followed by a stripper who was equally jeered. 'If ye don't cut that out, lads,' shouted the MC, 'I'll bring back the Irish comic!'

And yet he always came back for more. And more and more, until, by consent amongst his peers, he became one of the most successful Irish comics ever.

That interview was promoting Jury's Cabaret one year, so it was possible to watch him feed this insatiable desire for praise and love as, for a long time after the show came down, he wisecracked his way through sales of his tapes and books to the man from Oklahoma who just loved his jokes ('I was just crazy about 'em'), the lady in the red polyester dress ('I was hysterical') and the man from Delaware ('You were marvellous, Hal. I'm in fibres. Du Pont'), while the rest of the adoring queue looked on with anticipatory smiles on their faces.

And yet, although in Roach's view Maureen Potter shared absolutely this need for public affirmation, he repeats that like her mentor, Jimmy O'Dea, she was less a solo artist, more a team player. Even in her single spots she (or he) never strayed far from the characters they had created. 'She was the Lucille Ball of Ireland' – a comparison also made by Fred O'Donovan, Pauline McLynn and Anne Bushnell.

Interestingly, when analysing her talent, he lapses into the present tense: 'The magic of this woman! When she walks on to a stage a metamorphosis happens: people laugh and they feel good; they get excited just because of the way she walks on …'

He stands up in his living-room, back to the spectacular view, to perform an amazingly accurate impersonation of the way Potter used to come on stage. 'I have the Maureen Potter thing now. I have to walk on now and I have two minutes. It's the way you walk. The way you come on. The eyes. The hands. Everything about you – your aura. You have two minutes for the audience to decide whether they like you or not.'

He sits down again. 'The president loved her. Everyone loved her. You just had to mention her name to apple sellers in Moore Street and the glow that came over them – I never heard anyone say anything derogatory about Maureen Potter in my life. Now me, it's a different thing. I'm not lovable. I have to work for it. I have to earn my adulation.'

He watches for a response. Then: 'Don't be so quick to agree!'

It's a real gag, delivered with timing and panache, but (see above) only half in jest and, quickly, he gets back to the subject at hand. 'She doesn't have to work at it. She is there. Once she has them, she can now recite "Mary Had a Little Lamb", she can say anything, it doesn't matter. I think she's the greatest Pantomime woman star I've every known. She can take a script – it's the way she phrases things. She has beautiful diction, Maureen. What's more, she's beautiful. She's sexy.

'There's a difference between a man and a woman telling funny stories – and a funny man or a funny woman telling stories. Most of us can tell stories. But stories are the least important part of being a comedian. She does things we all envy to such a degree that we began to hate her. I hate her. All of us hate her. Where can we get it? Can we buy it? Why her and not me? She's so bloody brilliant – it's not fair. Why was she given it all?'

No one on earth (well, perhaps Mahatma Gandhi or the Dalai Lama) can be serene all the time and like others – the vast majority of whom merely hint at this – Hal Roach admits that, like normal mortals, Maureen had her moments too.

And star comics like to be in charge. For instance, she hated ad libbing: 'If I put in one extra word or phrase, hell had no fury,' he laughs. 'The *language*! No one could lacerate you like her. That's because you took her out of her timing; when she was on a roll, timing her single to sixteen minutes, she would permit no variation. Yes, she'd lacerate you, but then back in the green room it was "Come on – what are you having?"'

Also like others, he greatly admired, not only her nous on stage, but also her intelligence off it. 'She was also a very learned lady. All aspects of world affairs, an avid reader. She was very sophisticated actually – she had all these great attributes that all came together when she was on the stage.'

He agrees too that the private core was completely inaccessible except, perhaps, to her family and a fiercely loyal few, who would eat broken glass rather than blab about anything personal concerning their heroine. 'She was shy in many ways, you know – that's OK. A little shyness is a good thing. But I think she was always afraid she might say something people might misconstrue and Jack was always there to say "no".'

Maureen Potter's husband, he says, is as much of an enigma in his own way as Maureen herself was. 'I've never met two people, two personalities, anywhere in the world who were so different. He's an extraordinary man, the most untheatrical I've ever known. He liked me,' he adds thoughtfully, before adding the qualifying: 'she liked my timing and he was the same.'

Fred O'Donovan and the majority of others in the business believe that Maureen Potter could have been internationally 'huge' had she accepted some of the numerous offers she received to work abroad. Roach disagrees. 'Maureen couldn't travel. I saw her on American TV doing the Irish dancing sketch where she couldn't walk with all the medals. And she was congratulated by reviewers on being one of the most brilliant Irish dancers ever to cross the Atlantic.'

As one of a handful of Irish comics who has successfully made the transition, he speaks with some authority about this. 'The reason why most of our comics here have difficulty in America is our words.' He then reveals his own 'light bulb' moment: 'If a joke is good and doesn't work, it's not the joke. It's you. If a story is funny it should travel.'

Sometimes, though, it needs a little adjusting:

> Robin Hood was dying. His Merrie Men were gathered around him.
>
> 'Open the window so I may gaze for one last time at my beloved Sherwood Forest.'
>
> They open the window.
>
> 'Bring my bow and arrow, that I may fire one last arrow. Wherever that arrow lands, there am I to be buried.'
>
> They buried him on top of the wardrobe.

The Americans sat in silence.

Until – light bulb – he changed 'wardrobe' to 'closet'.

They rolled around.

It seems simple, but if you've been telling this joke for years in your act, the simplest things can evade your attention. 'I found the key to the mainstream. Reno, Vegas, it all happened then.'

To be clear, it wasn't just the change of words. Hal Roach works and worries his act until the timing of every gag is perfect. His instincts for 'reading' a particular audience have also been honed to precision. The Americans, brought up with Bob Hope and Jack Benny, responded.

Nevertheless, the insecurity of the comic is frightening. ('Listen,' a friend has said, 'if Hal wakes up at 7.00, and isn't worrying by 7.01, he'll think there's something wrong and that he will end up in a mental home.') 'Maureen's the most nervous of all of us. She's a pacer. She gets physically ill.'

They shared, he says, another trait: 'Why I've been so successful – Maureen too – we don't use salacious material.

In fact, he was once brought on to the *Merv Griffin Show* in the States along with comedian Eddie Murphy, whose stand-up material is very blue; it was billed as a debate between 'the cleanest and the dirtiest comedians in the world'.

Roach's gags are well worn but still work:

> The phone rings in the hospital.
> Murphy: 'How is my wife?'
> Nurse: 'She's in labour. Is this her first baby?
> Murphy: 'No. This is her husband.'

Like Maureen Potter's Christy routine, this is intrinsically funny anywhere.

> Murphy's dog died and he wanted to give it a decent burial. The local priest refuses to bury the dog but sends Murphy up to the leader of a fancy new denomination. Murphy was grateful for the advice. 'Do you think, Father, that if I gave them sixty thousand euro that would be enough?'
> *Pause.*
> 'Why didn't you tell me the dog was a Catholic?'

Potter introduced political and social topicality to her shows but, like Roach himself, in the most general, non-offensive terms. 'She's one of the few that could get away with eviscerating the great and the good. People like being mentioned, no matter what.' And in Panto, for instance, her political monologues before the finale were what kept the mammys and daddys sweet through the kiddie stuff.

Comics are very generous in performing for charity events and Roach, who has a son with special needs, helps to organise gigs too. He is deeply appreciative of the lifetime's help he received from Maureen Potter. Sometimes she wasn't feeling well, but she'd still say "yes" ...'

Was she a happy woman off-stage?

'Her happiness was her work.' He evades the question – an unfair one, since how could he, or anyone, actually know?

'I miss her. I know that ...'

It's a good one. Write it down.

⌒

Maureen Potter's personal assessment of the nature of comedy was similar to Hal Roach's and, of course, based on her own experience. 'The essence of comedy is timing and control – and truth. You hold up a mirror-image of themselves in front of the audience so that they can laugh at their own most secret faults and desires. There are only about seven basic jokes, drawn on by all the comics in the world. They are based around the most human of concerns: birth, marriage, death, friendship, love and hate – and in Ireland, birth control!

'What we forget, we comics who take ourselves a bit too seriously, is that the audience has only seen that performance once. You've been doing it so long that you assume that they know it as well as you do. But even if they do, they want it again. We forget that comedy is like opera, or O'Casey. People will go to see their favourite thing, over and over.' In later years, she tried to drop the 'C'mon Christy!' routines from her cabaret performances, believing they were tired and outworn, but the audiences felt cheated. 'They were furious. "What about Christy? Where's Christy? Do Christy!"'

So she did.

In private life she thought of herself as 'desperately ordinary. I just read and look at the telly and cook food that hasn't poisoned the family yet.' But she did know that on stage she was not ordinary. 'When the laughs come, I think: this is not so bad.'

Jack O'Leary tells a story about Maurice Chevalier and Barry Fitzgerald coming round backstage one night at the Gaiety to congratulate her. Fitzgerald offered her a lift in the taxi he had ordered. She accepted and they said goodbye to Chevalier.

But when she got in to the taxi with Barry Fitzgerald – remember it was his taxi and he was by then a very well-known international film star – the taxi driver turned around and said, 'I hope you don't mind, Barry, but I'll be taking Maureen home first to Fairview. I know where she lives.'

TOMÁS MAC ANNA

I never had the pleasure of working with Maureen Potter but my understanding is that she was easy to work with and most co-operative. Indeed, she hardly needed a director for her many solo projects.

I did know her but merely to talk with her on occasion, and of course to admire the performances in variety and cabaret. I never missed a Jimmy O'Dea Panto or summer show at the Gaiety – and I recall a theatre-goer in the Gaiety bar saying to me on one occasion that Jimmy had better watch out: that he had a rival as good as himself in Maureen.

There are many memories of her performances in my mind as I write: her Artane Bandboy and soccer fan, who lamented that the band didn't play in Dalymount Park; and the fondly satirised bout of Irish dancing, complete with black stockings and medals.

The Gaiety was her territory, beloved, as she said herself in all interviews; it enclosed her in a friendly, loving embrace as she stood on that stage – balconies, circles, gallery and boxes – a great circle of enchantment.

Although Harry O'Donovan did write for her, it was her talented husband who was truly her creative guru, so to speak. But hers was the performance – wonderfully confident, with that precious gift that comedians and clowns used to have: to play the audiences as if indeed they were the closest of friends and every individual there a familiar face.

This all-embracing intimacy was particularly evident when she performed in cabaret, when she was to all intents a next-door neighbour with a good yarn or two to tell about the foibles of people and things and especially politicians.

It is not easy to describe fully and do proper justice to her talent – not exactly that of the stand-up comic, but more in the style of the famous Parisian *funables*: open-air entertainers, with more than a touch of the wicked wit of the Berliners before (and after) the wars.

And she was an actress in several ensembles – no easy transition for a solo performer. I recall her fine Vanessa for Hilton and Micheál's production of Denis Johnston's Swift play, *The Dreaming Dust*; her performance in a more recent Abbey production of a Hugh Leonard piece, *Moving* (Joe

Dowling had the happy thought of bringing her, so well deserved, to the National Theatre); and in a conversation with her once, she told me her ambition was to play Brecht's *Mother Courage*. (No need for me to say that she was a natural for any O'Casey play – and again, thanks to Joe Dowling, she had that opportunity and might well have had many more; several parts spring to mind.)

I think it can be said of her that she was truly unique as a performer – as much Dublin's own as was Jimmy O'Dea – and her flair for radio equally that for the theatre; her ability to create other characters as if they were around her, notably the unfortunate Christy, hoisted into the air under his balloons.

Happily, our modern technology still enables us to see and hear her, but equally, any one of the many thousands who flocked to see her, including myself, will always retain the happiest memories of an artist – as truly she was – who comes on stage and serves just once in a lifetime.

FRANK MCGUINNESS

I'm sure there are many reasons to love Maureen Potter. I met the woman on a very few, too few, occasions. She struck me as wise and honest. It would have been a pleasure to work with her, as it always is to work with those who know what they are doing. If they have to be rough to get the best result, then I'm with them.

Maureen Potter in Pantomime provided lessons in comic timing. The fun – physical, verbal – depended on ruthless accuracy. Her range was stunning: the gentle, sympathetic weirdness of her old lady in *Arsenic and Old Lace* matched that of Siobhán McKenna; her appearance in the third act of *Juno and the Paycock* as Maisie Madigan announcing the death of a son – in Joe Dowling's astounding production – had the force of The Messenger in Greek tragedy. This great, funny woman who, having seen the joyous light, had also looked into inevitable darkness. Her sparrow savagery in *The*

School for Scandal had her own unique music to sharpen the assault.

All stunning performances – and yet I love her above all for *Annie*.

Maureen and Jacinta White in *Annie*, with Tom O'Flaherty, dog trainer, and Rusty and Sandy. Courtesy of George McFall

My English partner, Philip Tilling, had never heard of Maureen Potter. I decided, *mo bhéal*, and we went together to see the show.

That night, no one on any stage in the western, eastern, southern, northern or Martian world could come near her. Loving, riotous, wicked, covering the Gaiety like Columbus crossing the ocean blue, discovering gold in every seam of the material, juggling the precious metal with such demented expertise, before throwing it generously and constantly out to us. The woman could not be stopped. To say that by the interval Philip was impressed would be understatement. By the end of *Annie*, the man was shell-shocked.

As we were leaving the theatre, he turned and asked me: 'That woman – just who is she?'

'Maureen Potter!' I replied.

'She's great,' he said.

There was a silence. 'Very great,' he continued. 'Truly great.'

And I agreed entirely.

I still do.

Any assessment of Maureen Potter has to include the following from the poet Patrick Kavanagh, who found her foraging as usual in the old Eblana Bookshop. He walked over and patted her on the head: 'Do you know what?'

'What?'

'You're not a bad little woman at all.'

FINTAN O'TOOLE

I've seen raw power. I've watched armies march down the streets in the capital cities of military dictatorships. I've seen a dictator sweep past in his black armour-plated limousine and his subjects gasp in awe as if they had just seen the face of God. I've observed the heads of multinational corporations speak and heard their sycophants laugh at their awful jokes and look mesmerised by creaky anecdotes they've heard a thousand times before. I've watched supermodels strut in front of dazzled, hopeless men. I've been close to a great political charmer as he made a crowd love him. But I've never seen anything like Maureen Potter.

I always hated Pantos – the tawdry clichés, the forced jollity, the overwhelming feeling that the actors wouldn't be doing this stuff if they could get something better. I remember being at a particularly ropey one in the long interval between the end of music hall as a vibrant form and the beginning of a glitzy, prosperous Ireland when at least there was money to spend on the costumes and the lights and the sets. It was that period when there was nothing much left of an old way of having fun and a new one had yet to be invented. It was one of those shows that went on simply because parents and grandparents remembered their own childhoods and needed their kids and grandkids to re-live something for them. What was on offer was basically the warmed-up leftovers of half-forgotten lives.

It was the worst of times, too – a Saturday matinée towards the end of a run, with the excuse of Christmassy festive jollity long melted away in the early stirrings of the spring. I was there on my own, without a child to amuse or be amused by, and I was working. For some reason I have suppressed from memory, I had to write about the show.

The stale alkaline smell of half-chewed crisps mated horribly with the overpowering synthetic tang of cheap sugar. The kids squirmed and screamed with that peculiarly dangerous mix of utter boredom and the rocket-boosted artificial energy of a sugar rush. The adults were getting weary and fractious from the effort of trying to control them: mammies were starting to poke and smack, daddies trying to sneak out to the bar. The performers, God help them, were toiling through the Ah-hahs and Very-wells like flagellants trying to think of their reward in Heaven. Nobody was singing along with the sing-alongs.

And then this small, bespectacled woman, the kind of middle-aged lady you would pass on the street without really seeing, stepped on the stage and everything just stopped. The effect was as instantaneous as it was electrifying. It happened without warning and before the parents could tell their bored, demented children who this lady was or what she meant to them. They all just shut up, leaned forward and plugged themselves in to the amazing little powerhouse that was Maureen Potter. They were caught and held in a grip they didn't want to loosen but could not have escaped if they had wanted to. They were hauled in by the glitter in her eyes, the rolling cascade of her laugh, the comic wobble of her walk. They stood on her palm like Gulliver with the giantess in Brobdingnag and did whatever she wanted them to do.

I'm very glad I saw it because it was, perhaps, one of the last flowerings of a dying art. When Maureen Potter walked on a stage, she trailed behind her not just a dead Dublin or the nostalgic haze of the rare old times. What followed her was something from the countless ages of civilisation, all those millennia before audiences were tamed and confined in neat rows and taught to behave themselves in decent silence. She came from a time that stretched from the beginnings of performance to the very recent past, when audiences were rough and unruly and unforgiving and actors earned their bread by being so charismatic that they commanded attention. She brought into the theatre with her something of the street singer or the fairground tumbler who either held the attention of the passing crowd amid the raucous bustle of a market day or starved. It was a tough kind of magic, one that created wonder out of terror, magic out of necessity.

Part of that magic was a trick of scale. The physical eye saw a tiny creature, hardly more imposing than a gnat. But the mind's eye saw a genie who could fill the largest stage and make the most cavernous theatre seem small. She gave off an energy, even when she was old and stiff, that produced the kind of relentless momentum that seemed possible only from a much larger body. She displaced air in vast quantities.

Where did this mysterious power come from? I don't know, but somehow whenever I saw her perform I always thought of another great performer from the music hall age: Bert Lahr, the Cowardly Lion in *The Wizard of Oz*, who knew all too well how spineless he was by nature but who vowed to roar and roar like he had never roared before to 'show the dinosaurus/Who's king around the fores', if he *only had the nerve*. Daft as it may be, the Cowardly Lion's belief that The Nerve would make the small and timid seem huge and mighty made a kind of sense of Maureen Potter. What she had, and what made possible the transformation on stage of a small old lady into a magnetic and almighty force, was pure, unequivocal nerve.

This is what she communicated long before she spoke: the complete absence of fear. She wasn't scared of the audience, not in any microscopic fragment of her being or obscure recess of her unconscious mind. I never saw a flicker of hesitation, a flash of doubt, a waver of anxiety, a flutter of panic. And audiences, in this respect, are like dogs. They have an unerring nose for fear, an instinctive sense of where the mastery lies. Reveal your dread, and they will go for you – silently and in their heads if they are well-trained theatre-goers; openly and cruelly if they are not. Conceal it – or better still fail to feel it at all – and they will lick your hand. Maureen Potter made the beast lie down and be glad when she tickled its tummy.

Where, though, did that absence of fear – or, better still, that ability to create the illusion of such an absence – come from? Who knows? It's bred in the bone. It's some kind of genetic mutation, a rare disorder that touches just a few people in any generation, a gift and perhaps also a curse that creates an addiction to applause. But it was all the more remarkable in Maureen Potter's time, when a brazen, powerful woman flaunting her mastery in public could have been a disturbing presence. That she was, on the contrary, an immensely loved figure in an often cruel and censorious society, has something to do with the success of her disguise as an utterly unremarkable person with anonymous looks and a curiously ageless manner. Something, too, to do with the way the variety theatre acted as a safety valve for the escape of bad thoughts, its licensed jesters shaking their cap and bells at the prigs and the scandal-mongers to the quiet delight of the ordinary citizen.

Yet ultimately she was loved both for seeming ordinary and for showing no fear. We knew that she was no distant figure of fantasy, no showbiz icon inhabiting a dream world. She was one of us and she suffered all our inadequacies and failures and discontent, except, in the wonderful illusion she created, that she wasn't afraid – not of the craw-thumpers and the Holy Joes, the bullying politicians, the hectoring bishops, the voices that told her to act her age, the whispers that said a respectable woman shouldn't be making a show of herself.

What could we do but laugh at the cheek of her and applaud, till our hands were red and raw, the bloody nerve of the woman?

PART VIII

an
extract
from

Tommy
the
Theatre
Cat

by
Maureen Potter

Illustrated by David Rooney

Tommy was dozing in his big red chair. The theatre was empty, but on the stage he could hear people talking and, in the background, the sound of hammering. That meant they were preparing for a show, and as the days were getting colder very soon the screamers would be back.

Suddenly he heard a voice calling, 'Tommy, Tommy, come along please.'

I must be dreaming, he thought. Usually at this time the cry was, Get that cat out of here.

Then the voice again, 'Tommy, Tommy. Cat on stage, please.'

Tommy peeped over the edge of the box, and to his amazement the biggest cat he had ever seen bounded onto the stage. Tommy had never known his brothers and sisters, but often at night he looked out the windows and saw other cats passing silently across the waste ground opposite the theatre. They seemed to be the same size as himself, but this cat on the stage was the biggest he had ever seen. And it was walking on its hind legs! He almost toppled out of the box in surprise.

The monster was being introduced to someone Tommy recognised – the small lady with glasses who often moved into the room beside the stage, with the name 'Maureen

Potter' on the door. A friendly lady who always had a pat for him and let him settle down on her couch as long as he did not lie on her clothes. Once, in a kittenish mood, he had played with some ribbons and knocked down a head of hair, and the small lady got very cross indeed. But she was usually a very friendly person.

And she must be a brave one too, for there she was holding the paw of this huge cat. Then, music started up and the pair began to dance. Tommy looked on, eyes like saucers, feeling very small indeed. If this creature could do all these things, Tommy would soon be out of a job. What mouse or rat would venture in while a cat that size was at large? And to think it had taken his name too!

Everyone finally moved off-stage, and Tommy ventured out of his hiding place to get a closer look at the intruder. He saw the big cat go into a dressing room, so he settled down on the landing above to watch. Shortly afterwards the door opened and Tommy crouched down nervously, but only a small man with glasses emerged. The man left the door open behind him, and after a while Tommy padded quietly downstairs and peeped into the room. There was no sign of the monster. Tommy crept cautiously inside. Then he almost died of shock, almost lost several of his nine lives. The monster was hiding behind the door! Tommy was trapped. He dashed under a table and prepared to defend himself. But no attack came, and eventually, nervously, he peeped out. The monster was still behind the door, but he looked flat and very still. Perhaps he was asleep? Perhaps Tommy could slide past him to safety?

Tommy was just at the door when he heard footsteps. It was the man returning. Tommy darted back under the table. Then, in the big mirror on the wall, he saw the man take off his shoes, put his glasses on the table, and then ... and then ... he climbed into the cat! Tommy was horrified. There was a man in that huge cat! Was there a man in every cat? Was there a small man inside *him* waiting to get out? He opened his mouth very wide and stared into the mirror. He could not see any man down there, only his red tongue and shining teeth. How did the man get past those sharp teeth when he wanted to get out?

Suddenly Tommy realised there was someone looking at him from the doorway. It was the big cat, but this time it had the man's face – a smiling face.

'Hello, puss,' said the face, 'you must be Tommy. I'm delighted to meet you.' He put out a big paw and Tommy backed into a corner, snarling nervously.

'Does this frighten you? Here, I'll take it off.'

With that the man stepped out of the skin, for that is what it was. He laid it on the floor and said, with a laugh, 'C'mon, Tommy, have a good look at it.'

After much thought, Tommy sniffed at the thing on the floor and then touched it with an uneasy paw. It was soft and furry, just like the white rug in front of the fire in that nice warm room upstairs. He had got in there once but a large man with a pipe had chased him away, shouting loudly to his old foe, the cleaning lady, 'Get that cat out of here.' Tommy walked across the skin and, now much braver, began to shake and worry that big face and whiskers that had worried him so much before.

'Hold on, Tommy,' said the man, with a grin. 'That's my living you're attacking. Here, have a piece of chicken.'

He picked out a piece of chicken from his sandwich and put it on the floor. Tommy moved to take it and the man stroked his back.

'What a lovely coat you have,' he said. 'I wish I had it.'

Tommy backed away from the food. Was this a trick to get his skin? The man laughed.

'Eat your food. I'm not after your fur. We cats must stick together.'

Just then a voice below called, 'Tommy, Tommy,' and the man, picking up the cat skin, said, 'C'mon partner, let's give them a double act.' Tommy followed him cautiously downstairs and when they walked on stage together everyone laughed.

MAUREEN POTTER

off-stage

Maureen Potter was a fierce guard of her personal and family privacy and, outside of that family circle, no contributor feels she could be completely known as a person. Nevertheless, with a hundred loving fans now contributing what they do know, or feel they know, a picture begins to emerge.

Maureen with her sons, John and Hugh. *Courtesy of Jack O'Leary*

Maureen Potter and I had a unique relationship that stretched back over six years. The uniqueness was that, in those six years, we only met about six times, usually at first nights. And each conversation, a year apart, contained the same elements of information, repeated and confirmed, with just a few new nuggets then added. Thus, we discovered each other slowly and tentatively and, unfortunately, always with time running out.

At our first conversation, I made a complete show of myself. The problem was that I was overwhelmed – and so I gabbled on about how she was always part of our family, how at every Christmastime the arrival of the Gaiety panto-mime was almost as exciting as the arrival of Santa Claus, how we could all quote her funny lines, how much we admired her timing and her delivery and her looks and her asides and her ...

At this point, I think she had heard enough – and she did what I had seen her do so many times on the Gaiety stage. She held up her hand, palm towards me and then closed it as though she had snapped a fly in flight. I was silenced, just as I seen a cheering Gaiety audience being magically silenced. And she said, 'And when are you going to write a play for me?'

I was (as my father used to say) completely flabbergasted – and I could see her revelling in her control of the situation. It wasn't that I would not write a play for her, but rather my amazement that she was even aware that I was a playwright. But she was more than aware and spoke generously about my work until the bells announced the beginning of that first-night play and the end of our first meeting. Then she left me, saying back over her shoulder, 'And don't forget about my play.'

This jovial comment became her final exit-line at all our annual meetings. And within the following five years, I was privileged to slowly discover (slowly because this most public lady was one of the most private people I have ever known) what delighted her, what depressed her, what were her disappointments and what were her ambitions.

On one occasion, our entire annual conversation centred around the nature of comedy. We walked a common path here as we each compared notes on how we were always expected to 'perform' – how our private personalities were expected to match our public ones. And I remember her saying that if the shoppers in her local supermarket did not find her as funny at ten o'clock in the morning as they had seen her in Panto the previous night, their looks of disappointment would haunt her for days. 'If I didn't have them falling across the grapefruit in hysterics,' she smiled, 'they'd be nearly asking for their money back at the checkout.'

She was, I discovered, obsessively proud of her 'straight' theatre work. She would remind me of her performances in the plays of O'Casey at the Gate or of Hugh Leonard's at the Abbey – and when I once commented at how, as Maisie Madigan in *Juno and the Paycock*, she sat on a chair swinging her legs, she just revelled in the memory. 'Ah, did you like that?' she beamed. 'I'm getting smaller as I grow older – soon they'll have to lift me up into chairs.'

And I also noticed her tendency to divert me if I ever again began to lapse into another torrent of admiration. Once, she gently cut across me with: 'And do you like poetry?' When I said I did, she delivered the line that she had so expertly teed-up. 'Walt Whitman is very special. Very.'

That theme – and her favourite literary figures of Whitman and Nabokov – was then explored and, indeed, it continued into our next conversation as I wallowed in her range of literary knowledge. And later I was held enthralled as she praised or criticised a litany of writers, plays, operas, concert artists and, indeed, critics. (The latter with hilarious anecdotes, often ending with: 'Oh, I'd like to tell some of them where to go.') And thus, as the years passed, I slowly filled-in the jigsaw that was Maureen Potter.

At the end, of course, the jigsaw was far from complete.

As with all of us, there remained spaces that she ensured would never be filled and spaces that Time prevents anyone from filling. The real Mo Potter was known only to herself and those closest to her. The rest of us can only speculate or, in my case, wish we had been given a little more time.

Our last first night consumed us with laughter as we remembered some of the giants of Dublin's variety theatre. I gave Maureen my memories from the stalls and she gave me her insights from the stage. And I learned how, in *Tom Thumb*, the gentle Cecil Nash was almost savaged by The Performing Dogs, how Danny Cummins and Maureen once got their lines so criss-crossed that they hilariously reverted to the previous year's Panto – and how, pride of place, the great Jimmy O'Dea decided that Maureen would no longer 'feed' him the laugh-lines, but that he would now play them to her. And then, our first-night bell was again ringing and as we parted, wishing each other well, she, as ever, smiled: 'And don't forget my play.'

But Time denied us that as well. Or maybe not – if, in some Great Plan, I arrive up there to be greeted by Maureen and her stellar cast and if I find time to write that play for her – a comedy of course! And if some grumpy angel or cranky critic does not like it, can't you just hear her, with perfect timing and a nod and a wink to us, telling them exactly (with stage directions) where they can go.

And then from the gods will come the sound that graced her days here on earth – unbridled laughter.

ANITA REEVES

I loved Mo Po. She was my friend and my icon. Like so many others, I was thrilled by her every year in Panto and *Gaels of Laughter*. She was the reason I wanted to go on the stage: I wanted some share in the joy she so obviously felt up there.

Years later, when she fell ill during rehearsals for *Sinbad the Sailor*, I was asked to take her place.

Of course I couldn't. No one could. Mo's boots were far too big for anybody to fill.

However, together with Eamon Morrissey, I played that year and the next and I was amazed at how generous she and Jack were with their material, sharing gags and giving lots of encouragement. On the opening night, because *Sinbad* had an eastern setting, she presented me with a pendant that had been given to her years before by one of the performers in a specialty Magic Carpet act from Persia. I treasure it but have rarely worn it for fear of losing it.

It's so precious now, I'll probably never wear it again …

A few years later, we worked together in Hugh Leonard's *Moving* at the Abbey. Mo and I shared a dressing room and became great mates. She was in the best of form at that time, playing in a hit show with a fine company, doing what she loved. We had good times together, chatting about our lives, and getting to know each other better.

Personal stuff discussed in dressing rooms stays private – it's a showbiz tradition. You see, there's nothing like the clutter of sweaty costumes, dog-eared scripts, bright mirror lights – and nervousness – to make us tell each other things we'd never discuss in the cold light of the street; so what's revealed over the greasepaint and stubs of eye-liner stays there.

However, it's not hard to guess what women talk about when they're on their own: their families, their kids, the best way to get stains out of carpets (not!) So I don't think I would be breaking that tradition of confidentiality if I gave you one little hint about the kind of thing we talked about while preparing to go on stage during that show: how, on the night she first met her lovely army officer, Jack O'Leary, so tall and in such a great uniform, what impressed Mo most was that he bought her fish and chips on the way home to Fairview!

There were nights when we sang and danced and made each other laugh so much we almost forgot we had a show to do. On one particular occasion, we were belting our way through 'Mame' when we got our standby call. Mo said: 'Ah, isn't it a pity they wouldn't just leave us alone.'

However, it was no hardship to go on in such a pet of a play and so, as we did every night, we marched on singing: 'Olé, olé, olé.'

Thank you, Mo Potter, for the love and laughter.

NIALL O'BRIEN

I was never introduced to Maureen Potter and I never worked with her, but one day, about thirty years ago, she stopped me in Dawson Street.

This little person, who at first I thought was a child, blocked my way and skewered me to the door of St Anne's church and, in an unbroken rush, peppered me with questions so that I felt like the youngest member of a family being quizzed by one of my mother's friends about everyone in my house.

In this case, the 'family' was the Abbey acting company. 'And how are yez all keeping? How is Captain Bligh? And Harry and Bill and Vincent, and the two Goldens – I used to see Geoff a lot but I don't know when I last seen Eddie – and the two Micheáls, the Galway one and the Cork one, and Máire – I hear she's well again – isn't that marvellous, but sure how long will it last?

'I have to go now, but tell them all I was asking for them – and oh, by the way, I saw you in that Eugene O'Neill, you were terrific, but I wouldn't stay in that place too long if I was you –'

And then she was gone.

So – still not formally introduced and never got to speak to her either. Yet as she dynamoed her way up the street, you thought she was like a sherbet fountain, and wondered how such a small thing could contain so much fizz, then leave you feeling so happy.

Niall O'Brien was a member of the Abbey Theatre's permanent acting company, along with Patrick Laffan, Donal McCann, Des Cave, Geraldine Plunkett, Stephen Rea and Sinéad Cusack. The

Goldens (Eddie, Geoff and Geoff's wife, Máire Ní Dhómnaill), the two Micheál's (Ó Briain 'the Galway one', and Mac Aonghusa 'the Cork one'), Bill Foley and Vincent Dowling were the elders of the company at the time. The 'Captain Bligh' referred to by Maureen Potter was Earnán de Blaghd, the formidable and dour managing director of the theatre, notorious in his previous capacity as Minister for Finance for reducing the Old Age Pension in one of his budgets.

○

NUALA O'FAOLAIN

I only met Maureen Potter once, when I had the pleasure of interviewing her for RTÉ radio. She was very good, of course; she could do an interesting interview about her life standing on her head.

But when the recording was over and we were getting up to go, I happened to mention the late Marie Conmee, whom I knew and liked very much, and Maureen stopped dead and said, 'Ah, *Marie*,' in a voice so warm, so regretful at the loss of Marie, so amused still at the antics Marie got up to, so – there's no other word for it – *loving*, that I realised for the first time just how lucky Maureen's friends were to be her friends.

She sat down then and told me stories about things Marie, who was the Bad Girl, had dragged her, Maureen, the Good Girl, into. Weddings and parties absconded from, persons avoided in snugs, pubs left by back doors as persons came in the front doors, money acquired by unorthodox means and blown with great enjoyment, vast plots against Marie's enemies that collapsed because they were laughing so much.

They had a ball, those wonderful women of the Irish stage, even though they never had any money or real fame and did a lot of hack work. They enjoyed each other and were loyal to each other when those things were difficult for women outside Bohemia.

And when Maureen was around, I saw, they never stopped laughing. Even now I can hear her saying 'Ah,

Marie ...' and see her sitting down again, elderly as she now was, to bring her old pal back to life.

SUSAN FITZGERALD

One evening with Maureeen stays in my memory, although it was really a perfectly ordinary night.

We found ourselves in a pub in Pearse Street with our director, Derek Chapman, after a late rehearsal. As we settled up to the bar we were interrupted by a man sitting on a stool beside us. He was a sad figure, very, very drunk, with a trickle of vomit down his front, and he was determined to engage us in conversation. Although he was defensive, suspicious and potentially aggressive, I noticed that Maureen, far from ignoring him, treated him with courtesy and kindness, turning to him and sharing some passing banter. Suddenly he went very, very quiet and he whispered, 'It's Maureen ... Maureen.' His expression froze. 'I was at your shows ...' Then his whole face changed. 'I was at your shows with my mam ... We were at your shows.' And I noticed tears rolling down his cheeks to join the vomit on his jacket.

Now, it was a small moment, and perhaps no one else noticed it, but I always remembered it. Her innate humanity had wrought such a response in him that you could suddenly see the child at the Pantos all those years ago, and it made you wonder what terrible damage had so darkened his light. I think it's the secret of what made Maureen so magic on stage. She loved people, she connected and they connected right back.

I've been told that Maureen felt very nervous about the idea of going into 'serious' drama. I suppose she may have felt she did not have classical training and experience, but she had a very big spirit and an empathetic heart, wonderful powers of observation, huge energy and a strong work ethic, a killing sense of humour and lots of acting skill, and with all that going for her, she really needn't have worried. An actor's primary function is to communicate with the audience and so Maureen was on home ground whichever kind of stage she stepped on.

If you can find a video of Joe Strick's film *A Portrait of the Artist as a Young Man*, you can get a flavour of Maureen's versatility.

In this film, she plays Stephen Dedalus's unforgiving aunt, Mrs Riordan, and in one scene she fires up the family's Christmas dinner by defending her church's denunciation of Parnell because of his affair with Kitty O'Shea, a subject that divided many families around Ireland at the time. Gone is the nice smiley aunt we had seen at the beginning, singing nursery rhymes and playing pat-a-cake with little Stephen. Now, stiff and tight-faced, she sits at the huge dining table and mutters malevolently over her turkey and cranberry sauce, 'A traitor to his country! God and morality and religion come first.' Despite the pleadings of Stephen's mother to let the matter stop there, another guest, Mr Casey, comes to Parnell's defence, and Mrs Riordan's mutterings rise to a crescendo as she hangs him out to dry: 'Blasphemer, devil out of hell! We won! We crushed him to death!' And she storms from the room. Mr Casey is left sobbing, 'Poor Parnell, my dead king.'

In complete contrast, Maureen was a wonderful, blowsy Maisie Madigan in the Gate Theatre's famous production of *Juno and the Paycock* by Seán O'Casey. She caught all Maisie's exuberance, as well as her faults and failings as a poor woman with a cute eye to spot where she might pick up a few shillings. In one scene Maisie is invited in to the Boyle's apartment to celebrate the news of the family's legacy and as the evening progresses she is prevailed upon to sing a party piece. Well, no further invitation was needed. It was mother's milk to Maureen. By the time she got to the end of her song she had electrified not only the party but also the audience, and when the show went on triumphantly to take Broadway by storm, Maureen continued to electrify New York audiences who had never come within an ass's roar of a Dublin tenement.

Donal McCann, who played Captain Boyle, and who took

to very few people, responded instinctively to Maureen's innate professionalism and humanity; he adored her for her humour and her honesty, and I am told that during the play's New York run he would sometimes carry her up to her dressing room when her arthritis made it too painful to tackle the stairs herself. Amazingly, she never let it show on stage. She seemed to possess enormous powers of concentration and will-power once she hit the performing button. It must have cost her a lot.

I had an opportunity to observe this trait in her when I worked with her during the first Beckett festival the Gate put on in 1991. This was a brave and crazy project of Michael Colgan's to perform all of Samuel Beckett's nineteen plays over a three-week period. It was done on a shoestring but had a world-wide impact, for instance at the Lincoln Centre, New York, in 1996 and three years later at the Barbican in London. The project culminated in Michael's filming all nineteen plays in 2001.

Because some of these plays were quite short, it was decided to rehearse and play some of them together with the same director, which is how I came to work with Maureen Potter. She played alone in *Rockaby* and we both played in *Footfalls*. She began rehearsals almost apologising for her presence because she felt she knew so little about Beckett, but in that regard she could shake hands with the world, which was the main reason we were doing the project. We all faltered through to find out what the plays were supposed to be about, and we all contributed whatever ideas we had to help each other's performances.

Maureen's character in *Rockaby* is an old woman at the end of her days sitting at a window in a rocking chair, mesmerically incanting her desire for human contact in time to the rocking of the chair, finally rocking herself to death. It was almost unimaginable that Maureen Potter, with her astonishing energy and life-force, her innate sense of comedy, could negate herself sufficiently to create this desperate and lonely soul. Little by little, however, as her deep voice filled the darkness, the Potter persona dis-appeared into this sad figure.

And of course the good thing was she could sit down for the whole thing!

In *Footfalls*, this deep voice of hers interacted from out of nowhere with my character, a poor maddened girl who endlessly walks up and down the same strip of carpet, regurgitating some inexplicable hurt that was done to her in her life. The voice is that of her mother, who may or may not be alive, and indeed, come to that, the girl herself may or may not be alive.

As we worked our way through to the heart of the play, throughout all our flounderings Maureen was disciplined, supportive and good-humoured and, despite the pressure we were all working under, seemed very positive. I was therefore utterly astonished that in preparing to go on stage in *Rockaby* she was struck by a depth of terror I had rarely seen in any actor before.

Maureen in *Rockabye*, by Brian Bourke.
By permission of Mo and Patrick Sutton

I passed her dressing room a few minutes before she was due to go on and called out 'Good luck,' only to see her sitting there, her body rigid and her hands shaking, staring in dead terror at the floor. Her lovely gentle little dresser, Rosaleen, calmly attended to her, but knew better than to speak.

Then, suddenly Maureen got up, went to the side of the stage, walked on and was totally brilliant!

It was that will-power again.

T.P. McKenna

I can't remember the first time I saw Maureen Potter on stage but I do remember vividly the first time I met her.

In 1976, Joseph Strick was making a film of Joyce's *Portrait of the Artist as a Young Man*. Strick cast me as the father, Simon Dedalus. And – in a moment of rare inspiration for him – he cast Maureen as Dante, the aunt who features so strongly in the row over Parnell in the Christmas dinner scene.

This was the first scene we shot, a daunting task for someone like Maureen who had not previously acted before a film camera. I remember that when she arrived on the set, a diminutive figure in a Victorian outfit and upswept hair, I went straight over to her and told her what a privilege it was to have her with us. To my surprise, she was trembling and I murmured in her ear, 'You will be marvellous.'

We all sat down in our places round the Christmas table, and Strick told us he would do a master shot, which involved doing the whole scene in one take. The scene proceeded, and as the camera whirred, I could see that Maureen, her large eyes blazing, was getting bolder and bolder.

The row over Parnell and Kitty O'Shea grew to its climax; she rose from the table, turned at the door and – cheeks flushed and quivering with rage – in a stentorian voice said, 'Devil out of hell! We won! We crushed him to death! Fiend!' She slammed the door.

There was silence at the table, and then as one we applauded.

The weeks on set went by, we chatted and chatted and by

the end of filming Maureen Potter had become a friend. Every time I did a play subsequently at the Gate she always came to my dressing room with Jack. We'd then go to the bar, and her observations on what she'd seen were always acute and to the point.

For my part, I rarely missed a chance to see her in *Gaels of Laughter* at the Gaiety.

On one of my last visits to that theatre, while marvelling at how production values had improved over the years, I ran into Lorcan Bourke at the back of the Dress Circle and said to him: 'Potter's voice, it seems to get stronger with age.'

'You know why?' he asked. 'She sings everything in the *moinah*!'

'The what?'

'The *moinah*. The *moinah* key' – and a line from Cole Porter came to mind: *But oh the change from major to minor every time we say goodbye* ...

A few months ago, on the *Late Late Show* tribute to the Abbey Theatre, I was sitting right behind Maureen in the second row. We had met briefly in the hospitality room, and she had sat down beside me. 'She has got frail,' I thought.

And then, when her moment came, she had to be helped onto the platform beside Pat Kenny. But as the lights came up on her, thirty years melted away and the Potter of old was suddenly there before us.

The show ended. We had all been invited to a party but, as we rose to our feet, Maureen turned to me and said, 'I'm being taken home.'

In retrospect, her last words to me now seem prophetic.

PHELIM DONLON

During the late 1970s when I was general manager of the Olympia Theatre in Dublin, the management of the Gaiety Theatre very generously invited me, my wife Pat and our two daughters, Lorna and Sinéad, to the annual Pantomime, which featured the inimitable and unique Maureen Potter.

It was always a delight to admire and enjoy the high production values and the faithful adherence to the traditions of Pantomime at the Gaiety, and most especially to marvel at the astonishing phenomenon that was Maureen Potter, whose energy, versatility and commitment were nothing short of 'fantabulous'.

Maureen in Panto finale at the Gaiety. Photo: James D. O'Callaghan

Whilst as adults and as theatre professionals we invariably found ourselves entertained by the inventiveness and originality of the scripts and the lyrics, what remains in the memory in a most enduring way is the star's extraordinary ability to connect with the children and young people in the audience, which meant that they responded instantly and totally to her every word and action throughout the performance.

For our young daughters, the magic and wonder of the enchanting experience were heightened to outright amazement and disbelief when, towards the end of the show, Maureen greeted them by name from the stage. We were content to leave that mystery unexplained.

One year, as we were leaving the auditorium after yet another wonderful time, we met Lorcan Bourke in the foyer.

Lorcan was at the time a member of the boards of both the Gaiety and the Olympia theatres, and he was, in his own particular way, a very original comedian (but that is another story). Having accepted our praises and plaudits for the Panto in a suitably proud and proprietorial way, he invited us to come backstage and see Maureen.

We followed him along passageways, through pass doors and down many flights of stairs, pausing from time to time while he greeted various patrons, staff members and members of the company *en route*.

Eventually we were ushered into the green room and introduced to Maureen, who was having a well-earned rest between shows. Lorcan hurried away to speak to the stage manager about the haystack or some other urgent matter, leaving us to bask in the warmth of Maureen's smiles and laughter.

She spoke to our little girls as if she had known them all their lives, asking them what they enjoyed most about the Panto, admiring their dresses and generally making them feel that it had all been done just for them. I will never forget the fact that Maureen Potter was prepared to devote some of her precious rest time to talk to our two girls in such a genuine and unstinting way, demonstrating that not only was she a superb performer but, at the same time, a very special human being.

We left the Gaiety on a high! Maureen, thanks for the memory!

PATRICK SUTTON

'I shook her hand!' I was so excited to tell my mother. I was playing King Hrothgar in my primary boarding-school's production of *Beowulf* (!) and Maureen Potter was the guest of honour.

Her applause, when it was all over, was fast and furious and encouraging and kind and …

And then I met her. Shook her hand and she was lovely.

I kind of always knew she would be.

I decided to make my life in the theatre and that she would be my patron.

She became the patron of the Gaiety School of Acting, where I am now director.

RONNIE DELANEY

Only four minutes from the sea ...

Or so the brochure and the fifties holiday advertisement for the guesthouse or hotel in Bray, Salthill or Blackpool boldly claimed, before we ever heard of the Costa Brava or the sunny Algarve.

Maureen Potter's success, her humour and wit, was based on a timely sense of observation of the events of her time and an intuition to see the funny side of everything. Nothing was sacred. Her targets were mostly the politicians of the day and the more bizarre events that made the news – and naturally any athlete whose achievement merited national acclaim.

Fifty years ago the wonder of the sporting world was the running of the Four-Minute Mile – an achievement deemed impossible until then. Picture Maureen on the stage regaling her audience with one-liners about her recent holliers. The unforgettable waiter, the food, the view and her fellow tourists. 'And only four minutes from the sea – if you're Ronnie Delaney!'

Maureen and I were comfortable in our friendship as fellow celebrities in this theatre that is Ireland. We often met and latterly shared a very special experience. Our portraits were painted for posterity by that gifted young artist James Hanley, RHA. What I would have given to have sat in on Maureen Potter's sittings with James. It must have been great fun.

JIM DOHERTY

Maureen seemed to have the gift of total recall, with a precision for quotations, song lyrics and attributions which was pretty awesome.

In the mid-eighties I had the pleasure of contributing some music to Joe Dowling's celebrated production of O'Casey's *Juno and the Paycock* at the Gate Theatre. One morning our rehearsal was a little slow to start when someone (probably Joe) said predictably: 'Here it is, ten o'clock and not a child in the house washed.'

Theatre music, composed by Jim Doherty. Courtesy of the composer

Maureen gave me a nudge. 'Jim,' says she, *sotto voce*: 'why doesn't anyone ever finish that sentence?'

'Go on,' says I, mystified, 'tell me.'

'It's pure Dublin,' she says, then, slipping effortlessly into character: 'Here it is, ten o'clock and not a child in the house washed, not a piss-pot emptied and sailors in the bay!'

Not for the first time, I fell into the piano.

Is it possible that there is someone in Ireland over the age of twenty who doesn't have wonderful memories of Maureen Potter?

When asked to put my memories of Maureen together, I realised that there are lots and lots to choose from – all of which bring a smile to my face!

Superquinn's contribution to Dublin's year as the European City of Culture in 1991 was a sculpture by Leo Higgins which would represent the spirit of Finglas. The sculpture is a collage of two hundred hands cast from Superquinn customers, with the hands of older people at the base, supporting the younger hands of the next and future generations. We invited Maureen Potter to unveil the sculpture.

Maureen arrived with her husband, Jack. Young and old came out to meet her. My abiding memory is how everyone present reacted as though she was an old and well-liked friend. People were not actually queuing up looking for her autograph – it was not the sort of reaction that the normal film or theatre star gets. This was somebody whom they had seen or heard and whom they felt they knew personally because of the accuracy of her portrayal of the simple joys and humour of everyday Dublin life; and even if their son or brother was not Christy, they certainly knew at least one Christy on their street!

There was a band playing and, even though Maureen wasn't well, she turned to me and said: 'We can't have music without a bit of a dance.' So she waltzed me around the sculpture and inveigled everyone present to join in!

After I started Superquinn I was in the fortunate position that Charlie Walsh of Kraft Foods, who sponsored the Gaiety Panto, invited the family along each year, so that I was able seamlessly to keep in contact with Maureen's characters as they developed, while my children and older grandchildren came to know her as one of the funniest characters of Dublin. The greatest compliment I can pay to Maureen's memory is to say that in all those years I never left her without a grin and a chuckle.

In the late nineties I worked as producer of the final series of RTÉ's only successful (but critically lambasted) sitcom, *Upwardly Mobile*. We were looking for a lady to play the role of an eccentric local resident and the actor Niall Buggy suggested that we cast Maureen Potter.

Maureen came in to rehearsals and everybody immediately went on their best behaviour. There were no squabbles, no ego eruptions, no difficulties of any kind.

Maureen remained charming and professional and funny throughout. She was excellent in the role. Everybody adored her. There were no problems in pre-production – the first and only time that happened during my spell at the reins of the sitcom.

We recorded the episode in the main TV studio in RTÉ in front of a live audience, in which nobody had the slightest idea that Maureen had been added to the cast for that night. There was no dubbed laughter – the laughs were for real (and so were the occasional silences!)

We recorded the first few scenes. It was OK, a few laughs and some neat moments, but the episode lacked something. Maureen was nervous backstage. She was happy to be there, but it had been a long time since she had appeared in front of a live audience.

Then she walked on half-way through the fourth scene. The audience did a double take – then erupted into rapturous applause, clapping and cheering so loudly that they brought the recording to a halt. Nobody could do anything except wait. She couldn't say her lines. Those people gave Maureen Potter a ten-minute standing ovation before she had uttered a line of dialogue.

Eventually the applause faded and we recorded the episode.

I don't remember anything much about that particular episode now, but I will always remember the effect Maureen had upon all of us – cast, crew and audience.

She had the extraordinary gift of making people feel that the world was a wonderful place, and it was, as long as she was in it.

LARRY GOGAN

The Gaiety Theatre has always had a special place in my heart because it was on that stage that I made my first professional appearance in 1948 as a boy actor – I was only a baby! – in *Life with Father* for Illsley McCabe Productions. So I always get a thrill when I go backstage there.

Every year, when Florrie, myself and the five children went to the Pantomime to see Maureen Potter, part of the treat was that we always went backstage to see Maureen. She would have mentioned all their names at the end of the show and then they had the added joy of meeting her in person and having a glass of lemonade in the green room with her.

So this will be one of my abiding memories of this great artiste. She was the greatest comedienne I have ever seen in my lifetime. I always had a pain in my side after seeing one of her shows and yet when you met her she was one of the most down to earth and humble people you could ever meet.

Every time I think of her, I smile, and there are not a lot of people you could say that about.

BERNADETTE GREEVY

I am sad to say that I did not know Maureen Potter all that well, despite the fact that we were both not only Dubs but also Clontarfites and, in the general sense of the word, were both immersed in the world of entertainment throughout our lives.

In my opinion, Maureen's apogee professionally was during her long professional association with the great Jimmy O'Dea: the manner in which they sparked off each other in their immortal sketches attained heights of comedy genius that have rarely been equalled on any stage since. After Jimmy's death she went on to enjoy a unique career as a solo performer and was also very successful in straight drama.

The last time we actually met was in 1990, when we (among a handful of others) were conferred with honorary doctorates by Trinity College Dublin. On that occasion, as on any other times that our paths crossed, I found Maureen to be warm-hearted, charming and genuinely funny.

May she rest in peace.

AUSTIN GAFFNEY

On Saturday 25 April 2004 I sat in the front row of the Abbey Theatre as one of the adjudicators at the Dockland's Senior Citizens' Talent Showcase. The chairman of the very excellent and hard-working committee, in introducing presenter Kevin Hough and us to the audience, paused and told us that last year – the first year of their 'Talent Showcase' – Maureen Potter had been one of their adjudicators. There was a very audible sudden intake of collective breaths, followed by a deafening silence, followed by an instant tutti applause, which I'm sure Maureen heard from her heavenly state.

That was the love and regard which Maureen deservedly enjoyed right through her career. The love was palpable and it worked both ways because Maureen loved her audience, young and old. It was such an experience and a great honour to see and feel the magnetism while standing on stage with her at final curtain time.

Recently I recorded a programme for RTÉ lyric fm to celebrate the 150th anniversary of Percy French's birth, 1 May 1854. A wonderful Irish troubadour who once said, 'I was born a boy and have remained one ever since.' Change the gender and that could be attributed to Maureen Potter. I know what I'm talking about. She lived on Philipsburgh Avenue beside Fairview Church and I was born on Ballybough Road – just a stone's throw away – so I knew Maureen the girl.

She was only seventy-nine when she died yet when she retired, due to ill health, some people said, 'Lord she must be a hundred.' Yes, it felt like she was with us that long because she was always there growing up with us.

Her youthful vitality was always recognised by the

children, young and old, during pantomime. One thing that always amazed everybody was her capacity to learn lines, even extra lines thrown at her just before showtime. This talent she used to great effect at the end of every Panto matinée. She would be handed a long list of names of boys and girls in the audience which she would study during the interval and, without the aid of any notes, she would call out and welcome the girls and boys at final curtain time: sometimes there could be twenty or more.

Maureen in *The Problems of an Usherette.*
Photo: *James D. O'Callaghan*

Maureen, we will miss you, not only on stage, but also for your warmth and encouragement to all your fellow artistes down through the years. I am proud to say that I was one of those artistes.

May those 'Heavenly Lights' continue to shine wherever you make an entrance.

EILEEN DUNNE

'Keep your breath to cool your porridge,' we all chorused, on cue, but somewhat reluctantly, because we knew then it was all over for another year!

Funny the way those years melt into each other when we look back, but the Gaiety Panto was always one of the highlights of the Christmas holidays, very often a birthday treat for my younger sister Moira, who shared her birthday with Maureen on 3 January. Often Maureen read out the request, which my parents would have sent in, but she never mentioned the fact that it was her own birthday. We used to hope we would meet her around Clontarf and get the chance to wish *her* a happy birthday, but we never did.

Fond memories, but you know, when I think now of Maureen Potter, I think of her performance in *Arsenic and Old Lace* at the Gate Theatre some years later. Not having seen her in a straight role until then, I was stunned by her performance, and that of Siobhán McKenna. I had left my Panto days behind me by then, but now I'm back there with my own child, though now there's no more Maureen and it's just not the same ...

MARY FINAN

People often associate schools, music, fashion or jobs with different phases of their lives. For me, short-sighted and devoid of any concept of time, it is always people who evoke memories of days past.

As a child I related to everything Maureen Potter represented – fun, humour, big-heartedness and entertainment. She created a magical world that captivated every child's imagination. Thankfully, she was with us a long time and, somehow, her continuing presence seemed to reassure us that there was stability in the world and that those halcyon, childhood days really had existed.

For decades she has occupied a special place up there beside Santa Claus in the collective imagination of Irish children. He gave us the dolls and the train sets and then, as if life wasn't wonderful enough, we still had the Pantomime to look forward to.

Nobody understood children better than Maureen Potter. She played on our innocence and imaginations like a maestro on his Stradivarius. As we screamed our little hearts out we were filled with a giddy blend of fear and excitement until finally, to our breathless relief, the baddies were punished and Maureen and her friends were safe.

I am delighted that she was also a part of my daughter's childhood. It was wonderful to see her experience the same pleasure and excitement I remember so well.

Maureen introduced us both to the magic of theatre and gave us a gift we will enjoy all our lives.

JOE DUFFY

Maureen was always more than a comedian to us.

Imagine discovering in the Ireland of the early sixties that a woman the same age as your mother had a wonderfully successful career as a comedian and could mesmerise an audience (that she had been all-Ireland Irish dancing champion when she was only seven obviously helped!), who could perform on screen and stage – and then go home and be a wife and mammy!

And she was the mother of two boys the same age as us!

And then, to cap it all, our aunt got a job as the telephonist in the Gaiety – and who did she meet every day but Maureen Potter!

When it transpired through stories from our aunt that Maureen Potter was as normal and friendly as any mother, we were enthralled by her. And of course now we got tickets to *Gaels of Laughter* and the Pantomimes; these were our introduction to the world of theatre – we didn't have a television until the seventies.

If there is magic in the wonderful building that is the Gaiety Theatre, there was stardust on the stage when Maureen performed.

The mastery of her 'Christy' sketches was breathtaking: a lone actor on the stage with her imaginary and boisterous fourteen-year-old son as she endeavoured to get him into the *feis* provided unsurpassed comic moments. Even now to listen to the 'Christy' sketches on radio is pure bliss – Bob Newhart, eat your heart out.

And of course, with our aunt embedded in the Gaiety, we always got our names read out at the end by Maureen. I used to search for notes or names written on her hand or on the floor, but no prompts could be found. Because she had nothing but her memory. One night after her two-hour Panto performance, she managed sixty-seven names! And remember she did this after *every* performance.

And of course she asked us to tell our friends about the show or else 'keep your breath to cool your porridge!'

Well, the porridge stayed piping hot – as we regaled others about the Pantos.

And the same applies today, not a bad word heard or said about Maureen Potter: dancer, comedian, actor, wife and, above all, a mother. Just like the one we had!

PART X

That Was Then

Collage from Potters Bistro in Swords. Courtesy of Billie Barry

In the heyday of variety, stagecraft was a vocation and an actor caught in the green room or dressing room sitting in his or her costume was fined for creasing it. It was a time when under no circumstances were you allowed to wear the same shoes on stage as you wore off it. When the backstage people had so much respect for the artistes out front that they called them Mr or Miss and where they took the rap for whatever went wrong: 'I always used tell the younger ones, if you do something wrong back here they're the ones who carry the can. They're out the front in front of the audience. So you have to do everything perfect for them,' says George McFall.

This was a time when variety filled theatres and variety artists felt secure enough to play straight without getting nervous about the transition.

'Don't forget,' says McFall, 'that when those touring shows were out on the road in the old days, they did plays as well as the variety shows. And they did long sketches. A sketch to me is like a one-act play done in twenty minutes. Variety artists can do cabaret and can act, but it's very hard for an actor to do variety or stand-up.

This is probably why it's called 'variety'!

At the end, George agrees with everyone else that Maureen Potter covered all the bases.

And he reveals a secret. Although she got wonderful reviews for Annie – 'she was superb, she was marvellous in Annie (which, at six months, was the longest running show ever to be staged at the Gaiety) she hated it. It was different to straight acting; it was a musical and I suppose she didn't like it because she was tied down to everything she had to do. She couldn't let go; she couldn't let herself out.' However, although she confided in him, she did not complain. Got on with it.

Courtesy of George McFall

On a personal basis, what George McFall will remember most about this woman was 'her kindness and consideration. She was *always there for you. And when she met you outside, no matter who she was with, you were the important person when she met you.*

Conferring of the Honorary Freedom
of the
City of Dublin
on
Noel Purcell & Maureen Potter
in
The Mansion House, Dublin

OBEDIENTIA CIVIUM URBIS FELICITAS

Thursday 28th June 1984

Courtesy of George McFall

'I don't think anyone who ever met her ever came away without learning something.'

And she never forgot to send him a telegram for his birthday.

In an era when you could still send telegrams.

Last 3 January, three months before her death, Maureen Potter's phone rang. The caller was Billie Barry. "'What are you ringing me for?" Maureen sounded suspicious, even indignant. "I always ring you on your birthday, Maureen! Every year. For years, I've rung you on your birthday!" She was private to the last. It isn't generally known that she had been ill for many years, and not only from the crippling arthritis. Anyone who saw her at all knew that – but her death was quick in the end.'

First appearance of the Billie Barry kids in Panto.
Courtesy of Billie Barry

Billie Barry's 'kids' were widely known in latter years for their annual outings on the *Late Late Toy Show*, but they will forever be associated in theatre-goers' minds with Maureen Potter, both in Pantomime and in *Gaels of Laughter*.

Retired now, Billie herself lives in a sturdy post-war house tucked away in Marino, within strolling distance of Clontarf, where Jack and Maureen lived.

It's a charming part of Dublin, cosy, settled, a set from a fifties film or even a Pantomime: gnarled rose bushes, thickly painted pebble-dash, Sweet William in the borders of the small, railed front gardens. The kind of place where you imagine neighbour will never pass neighbour in the street without stopping for a bit of a gossip, and where in early mornings you'd expect whistling milkmen to deliver bottles from a horse-drawn float. 'It was the first Dublin estate. The

Germans built these houses just after the war. Any time you get anyone in to do any bit of work, the bits break on the drills and they're always going: "Who put up these walls? What are they made of?"'

Out the back is a wood-walled and self-contained studio, where Lorraine, Billie's daughter, carries on the family business of training children for the stage. (Another daughter, Joan, a dancer herself, is married to the singer Tony Kenny. The Barry dynasty is safe. And with all the other children's theatre schools around the country, including the three run by Twink – called AKTS – we will have an endless supply of potential stars.)

It is assumed by most people that the Billie Barry kids were with Maureen Potter from the start, but that is not the case. Other child groups preceded them. For instance the Oulton Kiddies, of whom politician Liz O'Donnell was one, did many of the shows, but when the slot unexpectedly became vacant, Billie heard about the opportunity and jumped at it.

Tellingly, before contacting the Gaiety management or even Potter herself, she first approached Maureen's husband. 'I heard it was going so I went to Jack about getting the kids into the show.'

A sort of legend was born and the 'Billie Barrys', as they became known, performed in their first Gaiety Panto, *Goldilocks and the Three Bears*, in December 1979 with Des Keogh, Rose Tynan, Maureen's beloved Vernon Hayden, Phyllis Allen and her Poodle Revue plus Fiery Daniels and his Magic Piano. (Scene 11, coming after those called 'Another Part of the Woods' and 'Francois Entertains', was: 'Your Chance to Sing with Francois and Woffles.)

Billie herself was fiercely protective of her babies. 'I wouldn't let hardly anyone near them'; although she did allow some exceptions: 'Aonghus McAnally could do what he liked. So could [she gets misty-eyed] Johnny Logan. Ahh – Johnny Logan …

'And *sometimes* Jonathan Ryan. Everywhere I looked, Jonathan Ryan was always taking photographs!'

She taught her kids respect for their elders. She was always 'Miss Barry' and she wanted them to call their show's star 'Miss Potter', but Maureen wanted to consider this. "'Let me think about it." Next morning she was back: "How about *Auntie* Maureen?"'

'Auntie Maureen' the star became.

'Respect is very, *very* important.'

Like Hal Roach, she talks about the obsessional nature of comics. 'Maureen lived from Panto to Gaels to Panto, always looking forward with very little in between.'

And she worries about Jack now: 'I don't know what he's going to do without her –'

Barry herself has had a long and fascinating life in show business. 'Papa was bandmaster at the Vice-Regal Lodge in the Phoenix Park; he always dressed beautifully.' John Clarke Barry subsequently ran three orchestras, 'all dressed up in Hungarian stuff'. And on the variety circuit, Billie herself and her sisters were known, with their mother, as Madame Lynette and her Dainty Dots; 'Mama was Madame Lynette and we were The Dots.' One of these Dots became Ann Hughes, a well-known contralto on the amateur opera circuit ('and one of her suitors was Larry Gogan's father!')

Billie herself was only five years old when she became a Dot. 'We worked for Harry Lynton in *Harry Lynton's Hippodrome* touring show. There were twenty-odd in the company and ten in the orchestra; we used five-pole tents and four lorries to carry everything. We generated our own electricity. People talk about running away to join the circus, well, we had loads of them who ran away to join us: Alfie Dundalk, Donegal Jack, Athlone – they were always named after the places they came from.

'And you know, people use the word "fit-ups" wrongly. For us the meaning was that you scarpered from the digs without paying the landlady – but that was others. That wasn't us. Harry Lynton was very good at paying and we were quality. When we arrived into a town it was like pop stars nowadays.'

The Billie Barry name still has cachet, and variety still has its fans: former Taoiseach Albert Reynolds, seeing a notice on the function board in the lobby of the Berkeley Court, bustled in unannounced to her retirement party to pay his respects – and stayed to chat with Maureen Potter, Maeve Binchy and all the other luminaries and colleagues come to say 'thanks'. And for the occasion, Jack O'Leary wrote a special routine for his wife to perform in her colleague's honour. The party was a surprise one and Potter stood up, waited the statutory minute or so while peering around the crammed assemblage through her over-sized spectacles. Then, with one hand shading her eyes, Apache-style, and in her trademark 'Christy's Ma' Dublinese: 'They told us to keep this quiet! KWAI-ETTTT?!' She was up and running. (Although, as Jack O'Leary said in his foreword and as is evident here, stand-up, unless it's an actual gag, with a proper punchline, does not translate well onto the written page.)

For once, the clichéd phrase *it's the end of an era* is apt for the death of Maureen Potter. Billie Barry says that, while there are 'some good entertainers' in the present day, 'They don't know Pantomime. Panto has to be worked. Like Shakespeare. It might seem over the top to mention Shakespeare in the context of Panto but it's every bit as skilful.'

DERMOT BOLGER

I never had the privilege of meeting Maureen Potter, nor as a child seeing her in Pantomime. Indeed the first and only time I ever saw her in the flesh was in the Gate's acclaimed production of *Juno and the Paycock*, when she played a relatively minor role and yet still managed to light up the stage.

By the time I grew up comic tastes had changed and, although Michael Colgan once broached the subject of her doing a straight one-woman show that I had written for the Gate Theatre, she did not feel well enough at the time to consider it. Therefore our paths only crossed once and even then more metaphorically than physically. But it was enough for me to understand the true depth of the affection in which she was held by generations of Dubliners.

Finglas, where I am from, was the location of the first supermarket opened by Fergal Quinn and some years ago the store decided to commission the very brilliant sculptor Leo Higgins to create a piece of public art to reflect the vitality of the place. Higgins' ingenious approach was to take casts of the hands of numerous local people of all ages and then to sculpt these hands into the shape of a raven – an ancient Viking symbol of the area.

I was approached to write a poem for the unveiling and, as a masterstroke, the organisers brought Maureen Potter to Finglas to unveil the sculpture, reciting the poem in the process. I was abroad at the time but the older locals I later met spoke of the occasion with deep affection. Maureen's presence, her aura and, indeed, her imprimatur had made the occasion special, ensuring that Leo Higgins' sculpture found an immediate place in the hearts of Finglas people. Her speech removed any barriers surrounding what might have seemed an abstract artistic concept because if it seemed OK by Maureen it was OK by them.

Occasionally now, I write in a small cell in All Hallows college in Dublin. Its long corridors are full of reminders of its past as a missionary seminary. Some mornings I pause to read a letter among the memorabilia that charts the history of the college. For me the letter sums up the closed world of that college decades ago and how Maureen Potter brought laughter into all kinds of diverse places. The letter is dated from the Gaiety Theatre, 6 January 1968:

Dear Fr Fagan,

This is to thank you rather belatedly for your very handsome and acceptable Christmas gift.

It was indeed kind of you as I thoroughly enjoyed my brief visit to All Hallows where I found my best audience for years. The sooner the powers that be open the theatres to the clergy the better as far as I am concerned.

On that score if you have any desire to see our Panto from the wings, as quite a number of clerics do, please do not hesitate to contact me.

Every good wish for 1968
Maureen Potter

DAVID BEGG

It was a shock when Maureen Potter died. She was around for so long that one assumed she was part of the permanent scenery of our world.

She was a major part of life when I was young. Apart from reading and the pictures, our entertainment was the radio and, together with Micheál O'Hehir, Din Joe, *The Foley Family* and Seán Ó Murchú of *Céili House*, she was much looked forward to. Her programme, which I think was on a Sunday afternoon, provided much merriment for adults and children alike. There was no real generation gap in those days. Her satire, which we thought was very cutting and hard on the great and the good, would hardly be recognised as such by today's standards. It was a gentler age.

Although I lived within twenty miles of Dublin, we had no electricity in our house until 1966. We had a radio operated by a 'wet battery', which the Boland's bread man, Jim O'Connor, used to bring to the garage to be charged. If Jim didn't have the battery back by the weekend there was real disappointment in the house, not least because we would miss Maureen's programme.

Then in the early sixties the first transistor radios came on the market. From our perspective, it was a great leap forward in technology, liberating us from the tyranny of the wet-battery charging. It also opened up new frontiers in radio, most notably Radio Luxembourg. I discovered Cliff Richard and gradually my dependence on Maureen and her contemporaries for entertainment began to wane. In the eyes of a teenager, the adventures of 'Christy' couldn't really match 'Livin' Doll' and 'Please Don't Tease'.

Still, Maureen Potter and her gentle humour are embedded on the hard disk of my memory, never to be erased. She was part of our formative years, brightening up an era when Ireland was very poor. It was an extraordinary tribute to her talent and personality that she could entertain so many generations over such a long professional life.

VINCENT DOWLING

A thorn between two roses you could call me in the early RTÉ situation comedy – *Me and My Friend*. The 'Me' was Rosaleen Linehan, 'My Friend' was not I, but a comic genius, the brightest female star of Irish Music Hall – Maureen Potter. I was the 'and' with a small 'a'.

The only thing I can remember about the series is that they wanted me to play Rosaleen's boyfriend, I was told, as a kind of 'Mícheál O'Bríain'. Mícheál was a marvellous, modest Abbey actor, who specialised in seemingly simple Connemara characters. Aye. Simple as the deep blue sea.

It was a double shock to read in Maureen's obituary that this short-lived series topped the ratings in 1973. All I remember about it was that the TV money was big, by Abbey standards, and welcome ... I can only assume that the reason I don't remember the details is that I was playing at the Abbey the nights it was on 'the box', or I was in America during the period it was being shown. This was in pre-video-recorder days.

Whatever the reason, on hearing that Maureen had died, I longed to have images from that show to look at. I suppose I wanted proof for myself I had acted with her, and with Rosaleen.

Well you can't have everything. I do have images galore of her, on stage, at the Gaiety Theatre. I'm pretty certain I saw her as far back as 1935 in the Pantomine. (Note: 'mine' not 'mime'! It was years later that I got that right.)

I think I remember her as Lord Mayor of Dublin – 'Alfie' Byrne – or is it that the little dapper, white-whiskered Dubliner was such a hero of ours that I recognised him in her, in those moments of her walking enthusiastically forward to shake someone's hand, on stage and off?

The thing I have realised since I started to write this memory of Maureen is that, though I must have run into her at a hundred places, a thousand times, always happily, only three or four moments can I conjure clearly. They are all on the stage, of course, but, before I go into those, I have a kind of riddle for you, and an odd little titbit. If 'a cry of players' is the collective noun for a number of legitimate actors, what is the collective noun for the great comics of Dublin Music Hall in the 1930s, '40s, '50s, '60s, '70s? King Jimmy O'Dea, Cecil Sheridan, Danny Cummins, Noel Purcell, Hal Roach, Jack Cruise of Bally-slap-a-dash-a-muckery, Mike Nolan, their side-kicks – Mickser Reid, Brenda Doyle, Cecil Nash, to mention but a few, and, the uncrowned Queen of Variety – Maureen Potter? I'm torn between 'a gag of comedians' or 'a thither of wits', but, whatever you call them, they had, as far as I'm concerned, one response in common, these intensely different, great clowns. Somewhere in any talk about 'acting' with me, or any Gate, Globe, Radio Éireann Repertory or Abbey actor, they'd say something to this effect: 'Oh, of course! You are a legitimate act-or! What does that make me?'

Yes. I've heard Maureen use that, too …

For me, the two great performance memories of Maureen are two great solo acts. Her imitation of Siobhán McKenna as 'Saint Joan', ending with – 'If the Bergundy-ans don't get her, the gin and French will!' And, still vividly remembered, an Irish dance solo in which she danced perfectly – jigs, reels, hornpipes and what have you – all the time commenting on how these dances had been developed from protective manoeuvres by the early inhabitants of Ireland, so that they could safely make their way through the millions of snakes infesting our green isle. And, she went on (with the addition of grinding heel movements): Irish dancing became the means of driving every last snake out of our beloved countryside into the ocean.

Not even *Riverdance* has matched the brilliance of that solo for me.

There was another matchless side of Maureen. Most Mondays of the first decades of my time as an actor at the Abbey, I saw the early afternoon live show at the late lamented Theatre Royal. We got in free, of course – indeed all the theatres and cinemas honoured an actor's business card in those more gracious years.

Often at the Monday matinée there wouldn't be twenty people in that huge auditorium, and the order of the day for the comics were tricks, improvisations and double entendres to 'break up', corpse or reduce to helpless laughter the other performers. Even the urbane pit orchestra conductor Jimmy Campbell was not safe from the slings and arrows of outrageous improvisation: Jimmy of the unnaturally black shining hair and pencil moustache, who maintained his overlordship of all he surveyed with a stylish baton. In the 'corpse-ing of others' category over all those years, Maureen gets my 'Oscar'.

On one particular Monday, in the middle of a sketch set in a Dublin street, the performers started to denigrate one another with this line of oratorical question:

'Who put the Miraculous Medal in the gas meter?'

'Who stuffed the tea cosy with the cat?'

The slagging got more and more outrageous, but it was Maureen who got the last laugh, 'corpse-ing' everyone including every musician in the orchestra. Appearing suddenly at an open window, high up in the front cloth, she yelled triumphantly: 'Who put the black lead in Jimmy Campbell's hair oil?' and slammed the window shut.

Game, Set and Match – Miss Potter.

My clearest image of Maureen is from 1989. It was on the Abbey stage in a fund-raising concert. I was one of two MCs and it was my good fortune to introduce Maureen. I made it short and to the point. When I came to her name, I turned, extended my right arm and hand towards the up right entrance and there I saw her, a little old lady standing in the wings, leaning on two walking sticks.

As the applause exploded in the auditorium she straightened up, walked bravely on, placed her sticks on whatever piece of furniture or musical instrument was upstage centre, turned smartly front and, smiling brightly, eyes shining and joyfully swinging her arms, marched confidently downstage centre to her audience, a young girl once more. When her act was over, she bowed, swung around, marched boldly up centre, took her sticks and exited, head high, upstage right.

What a woman! What an artist. Thank you Maureen Potter for the lessons, the lines, the laughter and the love for it all.

I know no one that is harder to imagine dead than Maureen. She was life, energy, talent and she will stay that way for me. I daresay for all who knew her.

If there is a God out there, I'll bet you 100 to 1, she is already Its Court Jester.

TONY Ó DÁLAIGH

When I first came to Dublin in January 1951, I visited more theatres than cinemas. There were two reasons for this. At home in Mallow, my father, originally from Cork City, regaled us with stories of opera and theatre companies coming to the Opera House and, while a film cost one and six, the gods in the Gaiety or Olympia and the back four rows at the Gate were a mere shilling.

So my first taste of Dublin theatre was when I went to see the Gaiety Panto with Jimmy O'Dea and the twenty-five-year-old Maureen Potter. I vividly remember a sketch that included:

J: You were in Spain for the summer holidays.
M: Yes. In San Jose and San Juan.

J: They are pronounced San Hozay and San Hoowan. When did you go?

M: The end of Hoon and the beginning of Hool-eye!

They recycled their sketches. One that came up every few years was set in a modern room in a bungalow somewhere in the West of Ireland.

On sighting Yanks, the room was frantically transformed into a caricature of a set for *The Playboy of the Western World* or *Riders to the Sea*: an old woman in a shawl smoked her dudeen next to a turf fire, a mini-*Riverdance* started up and an array of tacky souvenirs (including Brian Boru's skull) was made available for sale. When the Americans had bought up avidly and had left with their treasures, everything reverted to normal within fifteen seconds.

Maureen performed the official opening of one of the Irish Life Dublin Theatre Festivals when I was director. The sponsors hosted a lunch for her in their Abbey Street headquarters, at which she regaled the table with a host of hilarious showbiz stories.

I particularly remember one about the late John Molloy, who ended his career in San Francisco. Despite John's tall, cadaverous physique, he was, apparently, irresistible to women and many of his liaisons resulted in numerous paternity suits, not to speak of visits to various stage doors by ladies with babes in arms. One week, when he was playing with Maureen in Panto, there were two such visits to the Gaiety's stage door. (Tipped off, John evaded capture by leaving via the auditorium.)

On the Friday of that week, Maureen was in the backstage bar at 7.30, prior to going on stage. The elderly barmaid was busy polishing glasses.

Molloy stuck his head in, said: 'Evening, ladies!' and proceeded to his dressing room. The barmaid looked after him and, without altering her stroke, said laconically: 'There he goes, Old Silver Flute himself!'

It should have surprised no one that Maureen, when her Panto days were over, should have had notable successes on the 'legit' stage. Her Maisie Madigan for Joe Dowling and Michael Colgan in *Juno and the Paycock* at the Gate Theatre took her to Jerusalem, the Edinburgh Festival and, finally, Broadway.

She was excellent too in *The School for Scandal*, also at the Gate, and in Hugh Leonard's *Moving* – her only appearance at the Abbey.

The last performance of hers that I saw was at Clontarf Castle. She was clearly not as mobile as of yore, but the spark was as bright as ever.

John McColgan's excellent TV programme about her was aired again after her death; her radio programmes surely deserve to be aired again too – and soon.

There was only one Maureen.

GENE KERRIGAN

Sometimes, when we look back at someone's life work we see a rounded career, a succession of phases: struggle, success, adversity, triumph and decline. Depending on circumstances – talent, timing and luck – the various phases can be of longer or shorter duration.

We gain perspective, looking back, but we lose immediacy. When it's happening, the individual can't know whether they're having a momentary success or the beginning of a period of ever-increasing triumph. They can't know if they're encountering temporary adversity or if they're forever leaving a phase of success.

On the one occasion I met Maureen Potter, she had moved to the margins, having been for so long a central part of Irish entertainment. She could still bring in the punters, she had good years ahead, new triumphs as a straight actress, but her form of entertainment was now just one strand among several, and it was a thinning strand.

It was January 1980. We'd had a decade of bombs and

bullets, with another decade and a half of that to come. We were entering a period of economic decline and renewed emigration. Charlie Haughey had become Taoiseach a month earlier. Some of the biggest chancers in Irish life were girding their loins for a decade of plunder.

Vincent Browne's *Magill* magazine was still young when he got the bright idea that I should write a lengthy article about Irish comedy. It would be funny, it would harvest acres of showbiz anecdotes and it would tell us what – and who – made us laugh. It was a good idea and it turned out to be a pretty awful article, but that sometimes happens.

Twenty-five years later, I've had another look at the piece and it's still a lousy article, floundering and pointless. *Magill*'s readers were short-changed that month, but I had a great time drawing up a list of performers representative of Irish comedy. I spent several weeks working my way through the list, attending shows, interviewing comedians and having a grand old time. And central to the list was Maureen Potter, a childhood icon who could still fill a major theatre.

The entertainment business was – like everything else – changing slowly but relentlessly. For the younger performers, the cabaret circuit was booming. ('Cabaret' meant the same old singing, dancing and jokes, only this time in pubs and hotels where drink was on sale; when the audience was marinated the jokes seemed so much funnier.) People like Brendan Grace and Syl Fox were coining it. Newcomers, of whom Dermot Morgan was the best known, were struggling to find a voice.

For the older performers, not yet ready to shuffle off the stage, there were the remnants of the old music-hall tradition, annually limping back into view in the Panto season. For an old-timer like Danny Cummins, who shared an era with Maureen Potter and on the go himself since 1925, the year she was born, the cabaret circuit was alien territory; the audiences were alien, the venues unheard of. 'I'm told I'd go down a bomb in the Braemor Rooms,' said Danny. 'But, sure, I don't even know where the Braemor Rooms is.'

Alien and a little frightening. These were performers who knew every inch of the stages they had worked for so long. Now, earning a living required walking onto strange, stony ground. 'I'll do any form of entertainment, as long as it's work,' Danny Cummins said. But in cabaret, 'they want blood'. Danny's was a gentle comedy. It was painful to have to play it out in front of an audience calling out drinks orders. 'You can't be subtle or soft, you'd be wasting your time.' While we talked, he was in his dressing room, getting ready to go out on stage as one of Cinderella's Ugly Sisters and, as he powdered his face and strapped on a padded bra and a massive wig, he could recall exact dates he'd appeared in theatres on the British music-hall circuit ('3 June 1928, the Hippodrome, Manchester').

Then he told me about the emigrant group in Lusaka that contacted him recently, offered to fly him out, put him up for three weeks in a hotel, all meals provided, a slap-up holiday, and all he had to do was twenty minutes a night on stage. But there'd be no fee.

Take it, his wife said. Think of the publicity. 'My darling dear,' Danny told her, 'we can't eat what it says in the papers.'

Besides, Danny concluded, Africa was very hot.

Maureen Potter was less frank about the times that were in it, but she too was getting used to offering her talents to an audience easily distracted. The gentle entertainment that filled the theatres of Dublin, that brought busloads up from the country, wasn't clicking so easily with audiences used to entertainment with their chicken and chips.

Younger comedians such as Syl Fox had their audience figured. You had to know how to squeeze an emotion out of them – laughter, preferably, but whatever worked. For instance, in that pre-scandals era, towards the end of his set, with the audience well-stoked and emotions near the surface, Syl knew just when to throw in a monologue about the Pope in the Phoenix Park. It was called 'My Day to Remember' and it got a standing ovation. Syl knew his audience. 'Mention God at twenty to eleven and you'll bring the house down.'

Such monologues came from the music-hall tradition, but the newer comedians knew they sometimes had to go to the other extreme, depending on how they read the same audience. Syl said: 'It's 10.15 and they're half-pissed and if you try to do anything complicated they won't even listen to you. So, you give them a bit of the blue.'

Dermot Morgan had more complex ambitions, telling the truth through comedy – and with *Scrap Saturday* he would one day do that. Back then, he was known through his radio and TV gigs with Mike Murphy, but he still had to do the odd Sunday morning stag at a fiver a gig. He had trouble making it work in front of such a demanding audience. Cut out the complicated stuff, a more experienced comedian told him. Give them 'a bit of the blue'. So Morgan put together a selection of the bluest gags he could find and he still got slaughtered.

In the midst of all this, Maureen Potter and her generation struggled to keep a more gentle kind of entertainment alive. Backstage in the Gaiety, maybe half an hour before the evening show, while brushing her hair with manic energy, she'd carefully read the notes sent around to her dressing room. Would she please say a happy birthday to Siobhán, would she please welcome the gang up from Waterford, would she say hello to Tommy and Séamus and Maggie and Ken and on and on. And nearly three hours later, at the end of the show, after an exhausting performance, she stood out front and centre and, from memory, rattled off the long list of names, getting the names right and the places and the birthdays and special occasions, bringing whoops and shrieks of recognition from individuals in the audience, a magic evening fixed forever in a whole lot of memories. It's a trick you can still see on the Panto stage today.

There were other performers who would occasionally be dubbed 'a Maureen Potter for the 1980s', but it was clear that Potter would remain the Maureen Potter of the 1980s, and the 1990s. Her youth long past, she would never walk across the stage when she could run. The humour for the kids came in broad strokes, loud, big, colourful. Just moving from here to there wasn't enough: there had to be a little curlicue, a comic skip or a funny face.

For the adults, there was an element of political 'revue'. Looking back, it wasn't so much satire as an innocent glide across the surface of politics. More often than not, just the mention of a well-known name was enough to get a guffaw of recognition. In making fun of a recent Fianna Fáil conflict, Maureen Potter's tale of the Political Cowboys was delivered with a John Wayne twang. 'Bonanza Haughey has a real big spread – despite his jogging. He's got a real soft spot for Cheyenne Colley – the Bog of Allen.'

Jack Lynch was out in the cold, she drawled, 'and he couldn't even put on his coat because there were so many knives in his back'. That was as close as it came to satire. Such monologues made the adults feel like there was something there for them. In those more innocent times, that was enough; then Maureen could get back to the job of making magic.

And it is magic, that thing that happens between live performers and an audience. One of my clearest memories is of a curtain call at the Gaiety, the cast bowing, the music pumping, the applause persistent, Maureen Potter waving endlessly, and I turned to my mother and she was staring at the stage, totally entranced, maybe lost in her own memories of childhood, waving back at Potter. There's a joy and an innocence in such moments that you don't get anywhere else.

In the early years of RTÉ, they depended on established stage talent to provide drama and comedy. Initially delighted by the attention, by 1980 comic performers were in two minds about television. It got your name known, but it didn't make your fortune, and it had its dangers.

Syl Fox was making a very good living in Dublin, dates booked up months ahead. 'Of course I'd like to be a big TV star. It would get me known around the country,' he said. 'It would be nice, but TV can't make you. If you're a big hit you'll get lots of bookings. Then, sure, I have them anyway.'

It worked for Brendan Grace; at that time headlining in the *Cinderella* production in which Danny Cummins was an Ugly Sister. Having built up a name on the cabaret scene, and a good TV presence, Grace eased away from the circuit, concentrating on making records (later videos), filling theatres at Christmas and in the summer, in the pattern laid down by Maureen Potter and her generation. 'If you want to get people to come in here to see you in large numbers,' Grace said, 'you can't be appearing all over the place every night of the week. It spoils the magic.'

It worked for Grace, but TV had its dangers. One TV appearance ate up the material that could be sold piecemeal to hundreds of audiences over the course of a year. And if a good TV performance got you extra lucrative cabaret bookings, a bad one could wipe you out. 'If you bomb,' Syl Fox said, 'well, you're on a hiding to nothing.'

In the early years, RTÉ depended a lot on Maureen Potter for family comedy. 'Television?' She chose her words carefully. 'Sure, you could ruin yourself on television.'

Potter's big, loud performance was perfectly judged to reach every last seat in a theatre. She could react to the collective response of the audience, adjusting the performance as she went along. If a line didn't work, she could throw in a double take and rescue it with any one of the thousand well-honed 'ad libs' that such performers accumulated over the decades. And she came to realise that kind of performance wasn't suited to the intimacy of the small screen. 'It's a very different kind of comedy. Maybe, it's like stage actors when they do cinema ...' she tailed off '... project too much.'

By 1980, things had changed. RTÉ had already developed a reputation for handling comedy poorly. The one big success was *Hall's Pictorial Weekly*, and it's notable that it didn't come from a comedy tradition. Frank Hall was a journalist; his cast – Eamon Morrissey, Frank Kelly, Derry Power – were primarily straight actors.

The station wasn't good at generating new comic talent, but it recognised that the talent that had served it well in the early years wasn't enough anymore. Perhaps the television exposure, a stage presence in an intimate medium, didn't do Maureen Potter any favours, giving a dated, limited view of her talent. 'I used to do the Christmas shows,' she said. 'They don't seem to ask me anymore.' She was too polite to enlarge on that comment except to say, 'And I don't offer.'

Maybe entertainment wasn't any longer a thing of magic, encountered in a theatre once or twice a year. Now, we lived in a culture affluent enough to have entertainment on tap from television, in the hotels and the pubs. That was a transitional time, when talents like Dermot Morgan hadn't broken through and talents like Maureen Potter and Danny Cummins weren't quite ready for the curtain. But talking to them backstage as they readied themselves to fill a whole theatre with Panto magic, and in turn to feel themselves re-charged by the audience, Potter's wistful tone was unmistakable.

No one could say this wasn't just a slump, no one could be certain this was an era moving into its final act, but spirits were low. Out front, the colours were bright as ever, the noises as cheerful. Backstage there was a melancholy tone to Maureen Potter's comments about Christmas TV shows and Danny Cummins' wariness of cabaret. Talking about the decision not to take the Lusaka gig, Danny managed to see a positive side to the offer. 'It was nice to know that someone remembers, that the public haven't forgotten you. It's nice that someone knows you're good at what you do. That makes it worthwhile.'

GAY BYRNE

It was the memory thing that always astonished me: that trick she did, every night during the run of a Panto, of memorising during the interval the names of twenty, thirty or forty children in the audience, and then, at the end of the show, sending them all greetings. No bits of paper, no hurried scribbles, no crib cards, just an amazing feat of memory. And the excitement in our house when the names of our Crona and Suz (and their mum and dad) were mentioned from the stage. Maureen had the confidence to do that, night after night, after a tough day's work.

But she had no confidence about her drawing-power outside her beloved Gaiety. She felt at home there, safe in the place where her adult professional self had been born alongside Jimmy O'Dea; the space behind that proscenium arch was warm and familiar and she was as comfortable behind it as if in the womb.

Gay Byrne and Maureen, Late Late Show tribute, 1976.
© RTÉ Stills Library

I drove her home from a *Late Late Show* one night – it wasn't her own special tribute show; it must have been another, lesser occasion – and her old and trusted pal and accompanist, Thelma Ramsey, was with us. They were having a conversation, which, clearly, they'd had before, about taking a show out around the country. Maureen, nervous and suspicious, had grave doubts about there being an audience for her out there in rural Ireland and Thelma was trying to reassure her that indeed there was. Not only an audience, but a whole new life for her outside the Gaiety. I joined in and promised her that it was so, urging her to try it.

The upshot was that shortly afterwards she ventured as far as Mullingar or Athlone, or some such, to find to her amazement that they were waiting for her in huge numbers and that she was playing to packed houses. So much so that she then took herself further, to places like Galway and Sligo and Limerick, and found that everywhere they loved her every bit as much as they had in Dublin.

Arising out of that, my good friends and neighbours, Gerry and Carmel Houlihan, asked Maureen if she would do a trial season in Clontarf Castle. She agreed, hesitantly at first, but she was just as successful there. The Houlihans loved her and minded her and cosseted her hugely, so much so that the Castle became her second home-from-home for ten fruitful and enjoyable seasons – until the arthritis finally caught up with her.

I am so delighted that, even peripherally, I had some part to play in those years of happiness for her.

One sad note for us: it was always a little ritual for Kathleen that on Maureen's opening night, each season at the Castle, she would prepare a fresh flower arrangement from our garden and put it in the 'star' dressing room as a 'break-a-leg' charm. The week before Maureen's death, that bouquet was on Kathleen's list of things-to-do. She never got to deliver it.

God bless you, Maureen, for all the joy and happiness and laughter and gaiety. And thanks for all the hard work, which made it all seem so easy for the rest of us.

Maureen Potter, Queen of Comedy, was first introduced to the idea of appearing in cabaret at Clontarf Castle by her musical accompanist, Thelma Ramsey, with whom she had worked for many years at the Gaiety Theatre.

Her first show at the Castle was for a season of twelve weeks in 1983 – at least that's how long it was supposed to last, but the demand for tickets was so unbelievable, and the waiting list so long, we decided to cancel the following show in order to extend Maureen's run for a further four weeks.

Maureen, centre, at Clontarf Castle.
Courtesy of Clontarf Castle

And so, the woman who had tickled the ribs of the nation for generations took up almost permanent residence in cabaret here for the next ten years.

Maureen, to quote herself, loved working at the Castle. And in return, she was loved by all the staff and management. Each evening before the show, she would come in incognito through the fire exit, do a little dance through the Back of House, have a chat with the cleaning ladies, dance into the kitchens – a 'hello' to the chefs and maybe a taste of the 'specials' for the day – and then out and on to her dressing room.

Before each show she was very nervous and was prone to pacing up and down for some time, rehearsing each line.

After the show, though, things were different and she liked

nothing better than having a drink with other members of the cast and friends from the audience. The 'cabaret' in Maureen's dressing room was often funnier than her performance on stage!

She was very kind to the rest of the performers, especially young members starting out in show business.

Cabaret artistes were privileged to work with Maureen and there was always a waiting list to get on her show; amongst those who worked with her were Kathy Nugent, Tina, Harmony Suite, Joan Kenny and the Billy Barry Dancers, and Phyllis Meade and her Irish Dance Troupe. Her double acts with the late Jack Leonard and Val Fitzpatrick were hilarious.

Jack O'Leary, her husband and scriptwriter, was always there for her each night as if he were her shadow. He never missed a rehearsal and worked relentlessly for each show, with a new set of scripts, each one better than the last.

To celebrate her tenth year at Clontarf Castle, we created a new room and named it 'The Maureen Potter Room' and in pride of place we put a bust of the star. It was unveiled by Gay Byrne – and what a fantastic turnout there was in the Castle that evening to pay tribute to her. She was so pleased and said to us all: 'My bust is in Clontarf Castle and my heart is here too.'

She was universally loved. She had the capacity to make people happy. She pleased so many people for so many years and leaves us marvellous memories. There will never be another Maureen Potter.

※

She certainly found a new lease of life at the Castle. Take one night, typical of most, where the audience consisted mainly of large gangs of women, released into that free open space of camaraderie which seems to expand limitlessly when they get together away from domesticity.

'And a happy birthday to David …' shouted the warm-up

man, busy shuffling decks of paper fragments, all of which greet an
anniversary or birthday or special person in the audience. David,
apparently, was not present that night: the roving spotlight failed
to pick him out. But there was a great shrieking from one table.
'This is his mammy – his mammy's here!' and they pointed and
waved and tried to lift the mammy into the compere's view.

So when Maureen came on to do her act, they knew exactly
what to expect. The political stuff was topical, but they waited
impatiently for Christy – and for Bridie, the spinster bridesmaid,
who gets increasingly plastered and pissed off that she is never the
bride. 'They only ask us to be bridesmaids 'CAUSE WE HAVE OUR
OWN DRESSES,' Bridie yells before the sherry bubbles up and she
vomits all over the priest.

They loved it. They pucked each other and told each other they
could 'see' the priest as Bridie cringed and rubber-faced and
issued strings of MORTIFIED apologies at the empty air.

'Truth is that stomach you're holding in and that bottom
you've forced into that corset this morning but that you're going
to SET FREE TONIGHT!' she roared from the stage – and they loved
that even more, especially when she went on to have a go at
communal changing rooms and the sniffy young wans with their
wispy bras and tiny knickers who always SNEAK contemptuous
sideways glances at people like US.

Maureen knew her new audience.

∽

DAVID NORRIS

I only got to know Maureen Potter slightly towards the end
of her life. However, I remember her very well from her days
in the old Theatre Royal and the Gaiety, where she was a
perfect foil for Jimmy O'Dea and could do a Dublin accent,
with attendant facial expressions, better than anybody.

She mocked Irish life, public and private, but her mockery
was always coloured with affection. I remember in particular
some screamingly funny sketches, perhaps involving the little
brat Christy, where she would give a wonderful but

outrageously skittish version of pre-*Riverdance* Irish dancing. Her hands were kept rigidly down by the side, the face was poker to the last degree, the eyes bulging and the legs smacking out metronomically, then clattering on the ground with the iron-tipped shoes. There was no question of feeling superior. A lot of the people who laughed were people who had not only endured but also enjoyed Irish dancing classes and they could see the fun she was poking at it.

And then, of course, we heard her on the radio doing sketches either solo or with people like Danny Cummins. For she acted with all the great comedians after Jimmy O'Dea.

I also had the good fortune to meet her some years ago when I was appearing with Tony Kenny and a talented company in *Side by Side by Sondheim* out at Clontarf Castle. She came along to wish us well and kept us in fits with her theatrical anecdotes. It was very reassuring to hear of all the accidents that had occurred even to a great professional like Maureen Potter. Especially since even our show out at Clontarf was not immune from such disasters.

For instance, I clearly remember one evening during the run. The routine was that I remained in my dressing room until I heard Tony and the two girls, Joyce Teevan and Marian Duane – all waiting for their cue behind the main door of the set – snap this door open and, singing lustily, march out, closing the door behind them. At this point I would move into the passageway and position myself behind the same door, ready to make my own entrance.

On this particular night, when I got out into position, I thought my fellow thespians sounded a bit nervous. I couldn't understand this until I looked down at the door and realised that, when going on, Tony Kenny had broken the handle off. I was locked in the passageway.

Nothing daunted, I made my way out through a window, got in through the hotel kitchen and – since the set was dressed also for a Christmas show with a large chimney to accommodate Santa Claus – decided to improvise.

And so, when the light came up on the door and I heard

my cue, I simply slid down the chimney, landed on the stage and waited until the lighting technician had adjusted his focus and had swivelled the light around to where I now was. Then I continued my lines.

Maureen laughed like a drain when she heard this and declared that we were all true professionals.

The one anecdote I do remember her telling is one which I am sure everybody else has also told but it's a good one. When she was about twelve years old, she was touring with the Jack Hylton Orchestra when the group played to all the Nazi top brass in Berlin. They were all there, Goebbels, Goering, et cetera, all except Uncle Adolf himself. '*Heil Hitler!*' they shouted at the end of the show, extending their hands in the air in the Nazi salute.

Little Maureen, not to be outdone, clicked her dancing pumps together, shot her hand out and shouted, '*Póg mo thóin, Hitler!*'

She was immediately pounced on by the Gestapo and questioned as to what this strange phrase meant. 'Oh, it's "*Heil Hitler*" in Irish,' she said, knowing that they would scarcely be aware that what she had actually said was: 'Kiss me arse, Adolf!'

Full marks, Maureen! (She was also presented with some kind of Nazi triumphal wreath in gold and silver with bay leaves surrounding it, immediately and quite properly binned by her mother when it was discovered on her homecoming.)

You were always a brave and courageous spirit, Maureen, and wherever you are I am sure you are making them laugh.

NIALL TÓIBÍN

I first saw Maureen Potter on the Cork Opera House stage when I hadn't yet done my Inter. Cert. and she was already well up the ladder of success, though there was little between us in age.

Some eight years later, I played with her in Radio Éireann in the series *Meet the Mulligans*, based on the Biddy Mulligan sketches made famous by Jimmy O'Dea (and vice versa, of course). It was the tail-end of the Jimmy O'Dea era but the start of the even longer, brighter and, yes, funnier Potter era.

How happily I recall those days – rehearsals in the Phoenix Hall and drinking in Dick Purcell's (The Trinity Bar), a glorious sequence of hilarity and joy, far removed from the loosest definition of work. She was just great gas.

Yet I couldn't exaggerate how much I absorbed about the business I had just entered during those days. I had as yet no inkling that my budding ambition to be the next Olivier was to wither on the bough and that comedy, in the shape of variety, stand-up, cabaret, call it what you will, would be the mainstay of my subsequent career.

While I didn't work with Maureen again, except in charity concerts or tributes, I wrote scripts for her radio show, which was a staple ingredient of Sunday lunchtime for so long.

Radio Éireann had decreed that each show should contain a bilingual sketch – meaning, of course, an Irish-English macaronio – to assist the revival of the language. Ah well. It wasn't an easy commission, but I did what I could.

After some time, Fred O'Donovan, the producer, left a phone message for me, pointing out that the scripts were becoming less and less funny. Maureen sided with this view, for, let us be clear, friend or no friend, Maureen could lay down the law with the best.

I left a message, in reply, on Fred's phone, tartly suggesting that Fred should relieve himself of his bad humour with a successful visit to the lavatory.

He in turn acknowledged my advice, adding that it presented him with an opportunity to put my scripts to good and appropriate use.

'I walked myself into that,' I said to Maureen.

'You did,' she agreed. 'But you made a friend for life. He won the argument and can tell the story against you forever.'

Maureen Potter was truly a part of Dublin in the Rare Oul' Times.

Jimmy O'Dea was once given a dinner in his honour by

the Variety Club of Ireland. Rick Bourke, in paying tribute to him, turned to him and, with deep sincerity, said: 'We in Dublin often leave it too late to honour our own. And that's why we are honouring you today. My motto is, "give them the flowers while they can smell them".' Let it be written of Dublin that it didn't delay in Maureen's case, since she was given the freedom of her city some time ago. Rightly so.

While Maureen performed at Clontarf Castle regularly down the years, I made sporadic raids there and one of my greatest joys was to be told that Mo Po and her partner-in-crime, Thelma Ramsay, were out front like a pair of matching schoolgirls, Maureen's bright eyes gleaming brighter than Thelma's ever-glowing fag.

She was laid to rest in the old Clontarf cemetery, barely a hundred yards from the Clontarf Castle stage that, sadly, will no longer echo to the tapping of her tiny, shiny dancing shoes, nor indeed to anyone else's.

There will never be another Maureen Potter; let us be grateful to God that there was one.

౿

Perhaps now might be a good time to reveal the secret of The Litany – how she managed to remember the names of all the boys and girls who gave in pieces of paper during the performance in order that she might commemorate them in public at the end of it.

In fact, there was no trick or secret to it – she managed this feat by sheer hard work.

George McFall decreed early on that no names would be taken in after the first interval, 'because it wouldn't be fair to her to keep adding'. So just before curtain up on Act Two, Maureen shuffled all the pieces of paper into alphabetical order and she wrote them down. She'd start to learn them 'and I'd hear her. The way I'd hear her lines,' says Rosaleen, her dresser.

Maureen Potter studied those names after each exit into the wings, during each hurried visit to her dressing room, as she was being Velcro-ed in and out of her costumes. She studied intensely throughout the second half of each Pantomime, while keeping an eye on her cues and trusting she would also remember her on-stage script. She studied right up to the finale, when she went on and recited them as though they hadn't cost her a thought. And although the list sometimes numbered sixty or even more, she never missed one.

Maureen calling the names at the Gaiety.
Photo: James D. O'Callaghan

And she started all over again during the following show.

'She did it for the kids,' says George McFall. 'She knew they'd be disappointed if she didn't do it.'

Maureen's last TV appearance was in January 2004, on a special Late Late Show *convened to celebrate the centenary of the Abbey Theatre.*

So it's 1988 and here's Pat Kenny shivering in his shoes behind the scenery waiting to go on set for his first big gig as a television talk-show host. He had recently presented the Eurovision – yeah, sure, but that had been tightly and repeatedly rehearsed and well scripted; this was different. This was a live television chat show on which anything could happen. To make matters worse, he wasn't even a scheduled host but a last-minute stand-in.

On the one hand he knew that as a stand-in he had little to lose but on the other he did have something to prove to the powers-that-be in the hierarchy of Montrose.

The novelty factor on the (fairly short-lived) series *Saturday Live* was that each show had a different host presenter. Tonight it should have been Stephen Roche but a couple of days before transmission the champion cyclist had had to cry off.

Consternation all round.

Then: *Let's try Kenny. After the Eurovision he won't trip over his shoelaces anyhow ...*

Standing beside Pat that Saturday night in 1988, also waiting to go on as Stephen Roche's first choice of guest, was a diminutive, short-sighted little lady. She seemed as nervous as he and so, partly to settle her down, partly to soothe his own nerves, he chattered to her about this and that, about showbiz, the good old days, about anything and everything that came into his head. She chattered back. Sort of.

Then it struck him why she wasn't all that forthcoming: 'I'm terribly sorry, Maureen. You have to sing your song when you go out there and you have to remember the words. I shouldn't be talking to you.'

Through her over-sized spectacles, she looked up at him. 'I never remember the words.'

'You're joking!'

'No, I'm not. I never remember my words but every time I go on, they come back. I have to believe that. They will come back when I go on.'

And they did.

Sixteen years later, when the same Maureen was scheduled to 'go on' for the special *Late Late Show* celebration of the Abbey Theatre's centenary year, all in her immediate vicinity in the audience (except her staunch husband, Jack), struck by her failing health, were worrying seriously that this time she wouldn't, *couldn't* make it. Like everyone else who hadn't seen her for some years, Pat Kenny himself was shocked at how feeble she had become. 'Her fingers were so frail and bony; she was so shrunken.'

But that was superficial. Mo Po herself, more owl-like than ever, was simply sitting quietly in the front row waiting for her cue and somehow he knew with certainty that this time too the words would come back. He believed like she believed.

Maureen with Pat Kenny on the *Late Late Show,* January 2004.
Courtesy of RTÉ

Before transmission, there had been some talk amongst the production team that, in light of her seeming vulnerability, perhaps the presenter should go and talk to her where she sat. He had demurred. 'We knew she was in quite a lot of pain, but – and this has nothing to do with gravitas or age – Maureen Potter, the performer, deserved to be up there with the spotlight on. What's more, I hadn't a minute's worry about her. I knew she would deliver.

'And we made sure to place a speaker behind her seat so she could hear what was going on.'

Whether Maureen needed that speaker or not, no one will ever know.

Like most people in the Ireland of his generation, Pat Kenny was brought up listening to *The Maureen Potter Show* on radio; he saw her in the Pantomime; he saw her in *Gaels*. 'And later on I knew her round the place in the way showbiz people know other showbiz people, but after a performance of hers I always made a point of going backstage to pay my respects. Anyone working in any part of this world knows that no matter how many things you've done, or for how long, going out there is never less than an ordeal. I'm always grateful when people make the effort for me. And so I paid my respects to her.'

He was also paying dues: 'I always felt grateful to her.'

Because Pat Kenny believes that the 1988 *Saturday Night Live* turned out to be his unplanned audition tape for *Kenny Live* and led ultimately to the *Late Late*.

What goes round comes round: she was his first guest; he was her last host.

MIKE MURPHY

I didn't realise it at the time but I had the privilege of being present at Maureen Potter's final public appearance. It was at the special *Late Late Show* to celebrate the dawn of the Abbey Theatre's centenary year in 2004.

I was sitting in the front row of the audience with Jack, Maureen's husband, seated between herself and me. To tell you the truth, I was saddened to see how frail and drawn she looked.

At one stage she turned to Jack and I noticed she seemed somewhat agitated. 'Is she all right?' I asked him when she'd turned back.

'She's a bit hard of hearing,' he explained, 'and can't hear what's being said.' (Right enough the studio sound was at a ridiculously low level and even those of us with good hearing found ourselves under some strain.) He went on to tell me that her health hadn't been the best and she'd had to make a special effort to be present.

Then he confided that she was also dreadfully nervous because she had agreed to do a 'spot' on the show.

Suddenly, I began to get nervous on her behalf. She looked altogether too feeble – and bothered – to do herself any kind of justice.

Next thing we knew, we were going through a commercial break and Pat Kenny was introducing her to us. Jack helped her forward to the podium, returned to his seat and said to me with a confidence I have to admit I didn't share: 'She's going to be great!'

Then, when the show resumed, the studio lights came up and there she was, sitting beside Pat. Glowing.

When she spoke, she literally lit up before our eyes. It was as though every other studio light had dimmed to leave only one, super-bright spot to embrace her.

It was amazing. One moment she couldn't hear a word, then she had to be assisted on stage, so to speak, and now here she was, confident, lively, funny, basking in a torrent of affection from the hardest-bitten audience you'd want to avoid.

And then – she started to sing. To *sing* for God's sake! And there we all were, singing along, putty in her hands. As she finished, *she* applauded *us*, getting in first before we got the opportunity to give her the biggest, loudest, most heartfelt ovation of the entire show.

It was the closest I ever got to true show business magic.

PART XI

Exit

The actor Eamon Morrissey was also in the audience at that Late Late Show. *He knew that the cameras were going to come to him at some stage and was getting edgy about what he was going to say. Maureen, he says, must have sensed this because he can vividly recall the palpable waves of encouragement that kept washing over him from her direction. A few short weeks later, while touring with Garry Hynes' production of Synge's* Playboy of the Western World *for Druid Theatre, he and the company found themselves at Siamsa Tire in Tralee when the news came through that Maureen Potter had died.*

What he calls 'the difficult honour' of saying a few valedictory words from the stage that evening fell to him. When he had finished, in what he refers to as 'just a tiny token of how the whole country felt about her', the audience rose and gave a sustained and heartfelt standing ovation.

This is what he said that evening.

Today we heard of the death of one of the great talents of the Irish theatre, Maureen Potter.

She was a woman who to generations of Irish people brought laughter, joy and a little more understanding into their lives.

She was a wonderful comic and an actor of great ability.

Working with her, like many others, I learned that her comic energy was a complex mixture of talent, intelligence and that unknowable quality that made people want to watch her. She was a star.

Again like many others, when I began in the theatre I was the lucky recipient of her generosity, her encouragement and her good company.

Ironically, I heard of the death of Maureen Potter today just as I was going in to visit Ardfert Abbey.

I have no doubt, with her sense of humour, she would hoot at me about 'oul' ruins – how dare ye!' but, within that beautiful Abbey today, it seemed an appropriate place to stand and reflect on her great talent.

Indeed, it struck me that if theatre talent could be built in stone, how proudly Maureen's talent would stand on the landscape.

But theatre talent is as fleeting as a moment of theatre itself. However we do have a theatre tradition of marking such an occasion as this with an appropriate gesture.

So, on this her final exit, we invite you to join with us in giving Maureen Potter a last round of applause.

Ar dheis Dé go raibh a hanam dílis.

MICHAEL HARDING

I was standing on a bare stage in an empty theatre when I overheard on the radio that Maureen Potter had passed away. We were finishing a technical rehearsal for a show I was touring in. The people with me were dispersing for a lunch break. A few moments later, I was alone on an empty stage, in a dark auditorium, the only light being a faint blue in the wings to guide the performer on and off.

As a child, I missed Maureen Potter. Living in a small town far away from Dublin, I never shared in the gales of childhood laughter that warmed each city winter. And there were thousands of us whose drab January nights were never transformed by the glitter and dazzle of a Dublin Panto.

Even as very young children we heard about her. We heard the sketches on the radio; parents would call us to attention: 'Come in. Maureen Potter is on the wireless.'

And we would come. And sit in wonder. The comic voice. The quick wit. The abrasive tongue. Through the banister poles on the landing, we looked at the adults huddled around the radio. Maureen Potter. Like Santa Claus, she was a strange being, far away. And one thing was certain, even to us as infants. She was the real thing.

And because we never got to the Gaiety in Dublin, each winter we made do with the local Panto in the town hall. The bus driver staggering about in top hat and dinner suit, slurring a song that parodied the late-night revellers in the golf club. The local car salesman who appeared each year in a different frock, in a different story, as ugly sister or wicked witch. Sometimes he played Buttons, the common man, spitting asides at the local TD in the fourth row or at the pompous professional classes who came with their own cushions for fear the hard wood of the town-hall seats would offend their soft backsides.

We laughed. We stared. We exhaled in awe at the audacity of our own little world of performers, knowing that we too were joined to Maureen Potter by a powerful thread, because in that moment, we too were at the Panto. And in that moment before the ragged red velvet curtain was pulled aside and the piano and violin and drums struck up the opening fanfare, Maureen Potter was only an arm's length away in the dark. It was her voice we heard in the ugly sisters. It was her rhythm and timing we saw in the buffoon tripping ten times over the same banana skin.

Maureen was an invisible measure of perfection in Panto. A ghost in the wings of every town hall in the country. A mentor for every performer.

When the house lights came up at the end of the show, the hall was thick with sweat, body heat, plumes of blue cloud above our heads from the chain-smoking audience. The dingy hall brimmed with applause, joy and gratitude that in our little world a magic door had opened and we had touched the unnameable sweetness of laughter that makes every moment of anxiety bearable.

She was the hidden presence in the ritual. She gave dignity and status to the lowliest parish clown.

Standing on that bare stage, thinking these things in the faint blue light, I imagined I saw something in the darkness. Just a face. I saw it before me, like a great pumpkin floating in the dark above the stage. The spectacles. The startled eyes. The perfect mouth and head. Maureen Potter, as seen a thousand times on posters and in photographs. Was it a face? Or a mask? I tried to capture more detail. But I couldn't.

The thing about masks in theatre is that they hide

nothing. Rather, they reveal everything. The face is what hides us. When the performer puts on the mask, she reveals a deeper self. A mask takes off the face you have been constructing for decades and reveals the inner presence of the performer to the audience.

So I imagined her; a giant-sized mask floating above my stage. Spectacles. Startled eyes. Gleeful smile. And I realised that Maureen Potter had become a sublime clown. A buddha of theatre. Her face had vanished over the years, and what remained was a perfect expression, so that what the world saw was the inner presence, opened like a lotus to radiate its serene wisdom on everybody in the audience.

Then I let the image go and tiptoed towards the blue light in the wings, to get off the stage and back out into the glare of a spring day. And it struck me that, in some sense, I had met Maureen Potter after all.

⤺

Maureen's lifelong colleague Billie Barry missed the funeral because of a long-standing commitment to go to London. 'But I did get to see her in the funeral home before I went. I had a lovely long time alone with her, just her and me. She was lovely. In the black trouser suit and the white blouse with the big collar. What she wore during her solo monologues. You need have no fear when you die, they do you up great.

'Great.'

And so, finally, having attended so many funerals of so many loved colleagues in her 'gang', it was Mo's turn.

Some of these funerals had furnished her with bittersweet, even comic memories she revelled in passing on: for instance, following the instructions he left, Danny Cummins' coffin slid through the curtains in the crematorium chapel to the strains of 'Blaze Away' ('We'll make a bonfire of our troubles'). Then there was the funeral of the dwarf comic Mickser Reid, for donkey's years the 'feed' to Jack Cruise. She adored to tell this one because again it involved Cecil Sheridan: 'Jack Cruise and himself and a couple of other comics were carrying the little coffin. And Cruise remarked: "It's a very nice little coffin all the same." Cecil, who had also been part of Cruise's gang at the Theatre Royal, took exception to the phrase. It was insulting to their little friend. Some of the other comics disagreed. It wasn't insulting! The funeral came to a complete halt as all the comics carrying the nice little coffin joined in the fray ...'

There was nothing comic, however, about her own funeral, which, because it was Holy Saturday, was executed, not with bells and reveilles, but to the muted sound of a clapper and a quiet procession down the aisle of the church to the strains of 'Moonlight and Roses', the duet she sang with Patricia Cahill and forever associated with her in the hearts of her fans.

BRENDAN BALFE

Moonlight and roses
Bring wonderful memories of you ...

The song was written in 1925, the year she was born. It became the song by which we best remember Maureen Potter. She told me how it came about. 'I had long wanted to emulate a number I'd seen in the film *Presenting Lily Mars*, where Judy Garland did a number as a charwoman – "Every Little Movement Has a Meaning of Its Own" – and I asked Jack to write something like it. It appeared in the sixties in a *Gaels of Laughter* with Patricia Cahill. It appeared in the first half as a musical number.'

So now Maureen was a charwoman in a theatre, meeting with a young singer called to audition for a show. The charwoman lamented the dearth of good songs and singers, until the young singer joined her in a duet. 'And we never heard applause like it. We did it again and again in later shows, then on television. And I really did cry on stage when I heard Patricia's clear voice soaring through the theatre.'

They used 'Moonlight and Roses' at her funeral service in Killester Church on 10 April 2004.

Six weeks before that, I'd met Maureen in the National Concert Hall, where, along with Twink and the Lord Mayor, we were part of a panel to adjudicate a Young People's Talent Show, all from the Dublin Docklands area. She was in high good humour, despite being a little slow on the feet. I escorted her to her seat and sat beside her as we were entertained by dozens of talented youngsters. Many of them, she said, reminded her of her early days as a child star, over seventy years previously. We talked into the early hours and her comments were as witty and perceptive as ever. Not all comedians were funny, but Maureen was always delightful company, well read and knowledgeable in many esoteric areas. That talent show turned out to be Maureen's last public appearance.

Then 'Moonlight and Roses' was used as the theme for the tribute programme I presented on RTÉ Radio One on the morning she was buried. For that programme, I went back to an interview I'd done with Maureen in 1986, for the *Spice of Life* series saluting the great variety days, then already receding. She was reluctant to do an extensive interview, as she was innately modest, but I persuaded her that her absence would be a little like *Hamlet* without the prince. She agreed and came into the studio.

We talked of her early years, how she started dancing at the age of five with Dewey Byrne in the CYMS Fairview. She then moved to study with Connie Ryan, who had a studio over a garage in Abbey Street, Dublin, which necessitated her going to court in 1936. 'Someone was complaining about the noise we were making in the dance studio, so I had to go to the court and dance for the judge, to show how light on the feet we were!'

Connie did concert parties and she persuaded Jimmy O'Dea to come and see the young Maureen. O'Dea put her in *Jack and the Beanstalk*, 'as a fairy who defended the gates to the beanstalk. I also did an impression of the Lord Mayor,

Alfie Byrne, with a perfect little suit and a perfect little moustache – even if it did fall off and stick to the sole of my shoe.'

She worked in the splendid Theatre Royal on its first birthday. 'I was the candle on the birthday cake, singing "Many Happy Returns of the Day".' She continued with the production *Ali Baba and the Forty Thieves*.

In 1937, the manager of the Royal, Dick McGrath, asked the bandleader and impresario Jack Hylton to audition her. 'I went to the Number One dressing room and sang "Home James and Don't Spare the Horses". He put me on stage that night.'

In 1938, they went to Holland and Germany. Her story of playing for Goebbels and Goering and 'their fat wives in fur coats' is well known. She got lost in Friederickstrasse and was brought back to the theatre by a Brownshirt. 'They liked the Irish, even though we persuaded them that "Póg mo thóin, Hitler!" was Irish for "The blessin's of God on you, Adolf!" Connie Ryan even got off with Hitler's chauffeur.'

Back to Ireland, via England, she came. 'I never went through the awkward age, because I was constantly working. Then, when Jimmy O'Dea's "feed", May Tipple, left, I stepped in. One newspaper said I was "surprisingly good" in a sketch.' She was sixteen years of age and it was the beginning of a working relationship that lasted until Jimmy's death in 1966.

'His timing was immaculate. He was more a comic actor than a comedian. He could make you cry as well as laugh.'

Now, some people in show business are so used to answering the same question over and over again that they slip into auto-pilot with what becomes a stock answer. I felt I was getting the same old stuff about 'how marvellous was his timing' but I had heard from other artists that he was difficult to work with and thought perhaps she might come clean about him. So we stopped the interview and I suggested it was time to set the record straight, once and for all.

We picked up again.

What was he really like to work with?

'He never allowed anyone to call him Jimmy,' she said, 'it had to be "James A" or "The Guvvy" [Governor] or, behind his back, "The Little Napoleon". He could be very sharp. He loved mentioning people's names on stage, even dragging strangers up and into a sketch. He was a law unto himself, but he would upbraid others for doing anything like that.

'He also had the hardest hands in the business. In the sketch "Marrying Mary", he had to give me a clip on the ear. I nearly had the ear taken off me.'

As her career progressed into the fifties, she took on some straight parts in Shaw's *Androcles and the Lion* and Denis Johnson's *The Golden Cuckoo*, receiving great acclaim but remaining modest about it: 'It's easier for variety people to go straight, than for straight actors to do variety,' she said. 'Dancing was a great help, great training for timing in dramatic parts.'

Come the sixties, she was married to her scriptwriter, Jack O'Leary, and filling the Gaiety for six months of the year with the Pantomime at Christmas and *Gaels of Laughter* every summer.

Her brother, Jimmy Potter, also worked in the Gaiety for Eamonn Andrews Studios: 'The two most important aspects of Maureen's work were that she liked people and had a gift for talking to children without patronising them. Secondly, she has a phenomenal memory. She can learn up to sixty requests and dedications and deliver them on stage at the end of the show, without notes, without prompts. She realises it makes people feel special to have their name mentioned and makes every effort to do it. I've seen her talk for ten minutes without getting one name wrong.'

Maureen told me of an interview she'd heard with the actress Hermione Gingold: 'She talked about the drudgery attached to the stage. The cleaning of costumes, getting digs, touring, living out of a suitcase. And it's true, but we all realise that we're there to do a job – to entertain the audience. It's not their fault if you're dying from the flu, they should enjoy themselves. If we seem to be enjoying ourselves, they will enjoy themselves.'

She left the Gaiety eventually, to do cabaret in the Braemor Rooms and then at Clontarf Castle, where they named a room after her.

Did she mind being herself, rather than appearing in character? 'No,' she said, 'I thought I might, because I really loved the wigs and the costumes. But if you're any good, you don't need the wigs.'

Her days in Clontarf Castle, down the road from where she lived, were some of her happiest. It was to there her family and friends repaired after she was buried in Clontarf Cemetery, just around the corner. It was the end of an era – this time the phrase was correct. Maureen Potter, with her unique talents in singing and dancing, in comedy and mimicry, in acting and performing, was the last of the line of variety professionals who added spice to Irish life.

That 'tribute' radio programme closed with lines spoken by another variety artist who had left us some years before, Cecil Nash:

'My friends, the road we travel here is short, but it leads
    up to the stars
And on this road to Heaven's Gates you'll find no motor
    cars
But in Galway once, I met an old friar
Who whispered in my ear
That the One who came from Nazareth and walked by
    Galilee
Had saved a little spot above – for old pros like me.'

My final question in that programme – 'What is a pro?' — resulted in a perfect epitaph and a reminder of what made Maureen Potter great.

'It's to love your profession and, through thick and thin, to do it the best you can every night, no matter how you're feeling. To prepare, to do your homework, that is a pro. To do your homework before you go into a show, that is a pro. To look after your costumes, to give a damn every night. It's sometimes not even about the money, I think. I don't worry too much about the money, to tell you the God's honest truth. I've never really wanted to own anything in my life –'

She paused and smiled.

'Except a good pair of dancing shoes.'

As a final tribute from her city, the former Dublin City Manager Frank Feeley arranged to have the old graveyard beside Clontarf Castle reopened to receive her so she could be within range of her stage.

Anne Bushnell, who believed it to be apt that Maureen's removal took place on Good Friday, recounts the last steps.

Then, on Easter Saturday, we, along with her dear and loyal friends, Annie and Sadie Cuffe from Wardrobe, Rosie her dresser and the indispensable George McFall, walked with her towards her beautiful last resting place on Castle Avenue. Still centre stage, her final performance took place under a magnificent old tree. We stood near her beloved Jack, Hugh, John and her grandchildren to celebrate her life. We shed our final tears and wished her 'bon voyage' – and asked her to put in a good word for us with the Divine Impresario in the heavenly amphitheatre Somewhere Over the Rainbow.

We loved you, Maureen. Thank you for making so many people forget all their troubles the moment you appeared on stage or film.

Sadie and Annie Cuffe framed between John McColgan and Twink at Maureen's funeral. Courtesy of the Sunday Independent.
Photo: Tony Gavin

Asked in that long ago Sunday Tribune *interview how she would like to be remembered, Maureen Potter said she hoped that in the future people will say of her as they did of the drowned Seymour Glass in Salinger's* Franny and Zooey: *"'He was the kind of man you'd send to look at horses." That's the kind of woman I want to be.'*

And she was certainly the kind of woman who would have appreciated Anne Bushnell's final gag:

She was removed on Good Friday and buried on Easter Saturday. With her impeccable timing, who knows what happened on Easter Sunday?

Maureen and Jack O'Leary leaving RTÉ after her last television appearance. Courtesy of RTÉ

Courtesy of Billie Barry

Acknowledgements

First I must thank all the contributors, especially those who felt they did not want to write a tribute but who kindly agreed to be interviewed. Hal Roach, Fred O'Donovan, Pat Kenny, Billie Barry, Annie and Sadie Cuffe, Rosaleen Walsh, George McFall and Mamie Eakins could not have been more generous with their time.

Many colleagues lent treasured personal memorabilia – for instance, Barbara Brennan, Billie Barry, George McFall, Fred O'Donovan, James Hanley and Patrick Sutton.

John McColgan and Paula Burke of Abhann Productions, who produced the memorable 'celebration of Maureen Potter's career' concert at the Gaiety Theatre on 18 January 1999 were astonishingly helpful, as was Lucy McKeever of the Abbey Theatre Press Office.

I would also like to thank Marie Sheahan, C.J. Haughey's personal secretary, for her unavailing courtesy – and in the same vein, Samantha Traynor, who assists the Gaiety director John Costigan. Anita Reeves and her husband, Julian Erskine, were kind too, as were Martin Fahy, Kevin Hough and Bríd Dukes. Great support is also acknowledged from Collette Wallace, Pearl Quinn, Jim Jennings and Tom Holton from RTÉ, John Spain from the *Irish Independent*, Conor Doyle and The Irish Theatre Archive, Fred O'Callaghan and photographers Tom Lawlor and Michael O'Reilly.

The idea for this book originated with Joseph Hoban, PR and marketing director of New Island, and it has been a pleasure to work with him, with Emma Dunne, editorial manager, and with Fidelma Slattery, production manager. And of course, thanks also to Edwin Higel, the publisher, who ran with the notion from the moment it was put to him.

The project would not have been attempted at all without the acceptance and co-operation of Maureen's widower, Jack O'Leary. Although mired in the early, bewildering days of grieving for his wonderful wife, this most private of men nevertheless readily gave us his blessing and allowed us to reproduce some of his most treasured family photographs.

Profound thanks to all.

Author Index

Ahern, Bertie, T.D., Taoiseach of Ireland 3
Balfe, Brendan, broadcaster 255
Barnes, Ben, artistic director, Abbey Theatre 102
Barry, Billie, choreographer, founder Billie Barry Kids 216
Bartley, Jim, actor 115
Begg, David, general secretary ICTU 221
Behan, John, sculptor 77
Binchy, Maeve, author 25
Bolger, Dermot, novelist, poet 219
Bourke, Fergus, sculptor 108
Brennan, Barbara, actor 13
Bruton, John, T.D., EU ambassador to the US 23
Bushnell, Anne, singer 148, 260, 261
Byrne, Gay, broadcaster 233
Conlon-McKenna, Marita, author. 65
Creedon, John, broadcaster 69
Cronin, Anthony, poet vii
Cuffe, Annie, former wardrobe mistress, Gaiety Theatre 124
Cuffe, Sadie, former wardrobe mistress, Gaiety Theatre 123
Delaney Ronnie, Olympian 200
De Valera, Síle, T.D., former Minister for Arts 19
Doherty, Jim, musician, composer 200
Donlon, Phelim, arts management consultant 197
Dowling, Joe, theatre producer/director 92
Dowling, Vincent, actor/director, playwright 222
Duffy, Joe, broadcaster, journalist 208
Dukes, Bríd, director, Civic Theatre, Tallaght 104
Dunne, Eileen, newscaster, RTÉ 207
Dunne, John, chairman, IDA 23
Eakins, Mamie (Browne), school pal of Maureen Potter 33
Erskine, Julian, producer 139
Fahy, Martin, former general manager, Abbey Theatre 99
Farrell, Bernard, playwright 186
Finan, Mary, chairman Gate Theatre 207
Fitzgerald, Susan, actor 192
Gaffney, Austin, singer 205
Gogan, Larry, broadcaster 204

Grace, Brendan, comedian   116
Greevy, Bernadette, director Anna Livia
    International Opera Festival   204
Hanley, James, artist   5
Hardiman, Adrian, Judge of the Supreme Court   22
Harding, Michael, playwright   252
Haughey, Charles, former Taoiseach of Ireland   30
Healy, Eithne, chairman, Abbey Theatre   57
Hough, Kevin, radio producer/presenter   138
Houlihan, Gerry, proprietor, Clontarf Castle   236
Hussey, Gemma, former Minister for Education   76
Kavanagh, John, actor   117
Kelly, David, actor   28
Kenny, Pat, broadcaster   243
Kenny, Tony, entertainer   151
Keogh, Garrett, actor   49
Kerrigan, Gene, journalist.   227
Lawlor, Barbara, realtor (Canada)   144
Leonard, Hugh, playwright, novelist   8, 9
Lundberg, Gerry, publicist   136
Mac Anna, Ferdia, writer   203
Mac Anna, Tomás, former artistic director, Abbey Theatre   168
McColgan, John, producer   102
McFall, George, former stage manager Gaiety Theatre   38, 39, 141
McGuinness, Frank, playwright   170
McKenna, T.P., actor   196
McLynn, Pauline, author, actor   45
McManus, Liz, T.D., deputy leader, Labour Party   20
McWeeney, Myles, journalist   141
Maxi (Irene McCoubrey), broadcaster   143
Morrissey, Eamon, actor   251
Murphy, Mike, broadcaster, businessman   246
Norris, David, Senator   238
O'Brien, Niall, actor   190
O'Connor, Joyce, president, National College of Ireland   75
O'Conor, John, concert pianist   133
Ó Dálaigh, Tony, arts consultant   225
O'Donnell, Liz, T.D., Progressive Democrats   134
O Donoghue, John, T.D., former Minister for Arts   18
O'Donovan, Fred, impresario   40–42,85

O'Faolain, Nuala, author, journalist 191
O'Flanagan, Sheila, author 71
O'Kelly, Emer, theatre critic, columnist 153
O'Kelly, Donal, actor, playwright 61
O'Leary, Jack, widower of Maureen Potter ix
O'Reilly, Tony, businessman 24
O'Toole, Fintan, drama critic and columnist, *The Irish Times* 172
Parkinson, Siobhán, author 48
Plunkett, Geraldine, actor 118
Purcell, Deirdre, author 32
Quinn, Feargal, Senator, buyer 202
Reeves, Anita, actor 188
Reynolds, Kevin, radio producer, RTÉ 78
Roach, Hal, comedian 159
Ryan, Jonathan, actor, voice-over artist 111
Ryan, Phyllis, producer, Gemini Productions 105
Sargent, Trevor, T.D. leader, Green Party 24
Scanlan, Patricia, author 73
Sutton, Patrick, director, Gaiety School of Acting 199
Tommy the Theatre Cat, creation of Maureen Potter 177
Tóibín, Niall, actor 240
Twink, (Adèle Kingstage performer, director, AKTS
Theatre Schools 145
Walsh, Rosaleen, former personal dresser, Maureen Potter 123
Webb, Sarah, author 70